The Art of The Chinese Cookery

BY JOAN SHIH

Dear Erika,

Please enjoy!

Joan Shih   4-8-2003

極
佳
墨

Authentic and Healthful Recipes from My Cooking School

The Art of The Chinese Cookery

BY JOAN SHIH

Authentic and Healthful Recipes from My Cooking School

Copyright © 2001
The Chinese Cookery, Inc.
14209 Sturtevant Road
Silver Spring, Maryland 20905
301-236-5311
email: ChineseCookery@aol.com

Library of Congress Catalog Number: 2001-135516
ISBN: 0-9712869-0-6

On-site cooking class food photography
and Chinese calligraphy by Joan Shih

Edited, Designed, and Manufactured by
Favorite Recipes® Press
an imprint of

P.O. Box 305142
Nashville, Tennessee 37230
800-358-0560

Art Director: Steve Newman
Designer: Jim Scott
Editor: Georgia Brazil
Project Coordinator: Mary Wilson

Manufactured in the United States of America

First Printing: 2001   7,500 copies

Nutritional information was prepared by Joan Shih, the author, and
was calculated according to information and guidelines provided by the
United States Department of Agriculture.

All rights reserved. No part of this book may be reproduced or transmitted
in any form or by any means, electronic or mechanical, including photocopying,
recording, or by any information storage and retrieval system, without prior
written permission from the publisher.

About The Author

J oan Shih, the owner and the director of The Chinese Cookery, Inc., is originally from Taiwan. She received a full scholarship from Saint Mary College, Xavier, Kansas, where she studied pre-medicine and graduated with degrees in both chemistry and medical technology. Later, she returned to Taiwan to study Chinese cuisine and graduated with a certificate. She has written and developed recipes and designed the textbook for her eight levels of instruction in Chinese cuisine.

Besides teaching at her own cooking school, she has presented Chinese cooking demonstrations on local network and cable television shows including CBS's Morning Break Show, NBC's Fred Thomas in the Morning, UPN's Eye on Washington, and Cable-Fairfax Magazine. She has been invited to talk on the subject of healthful food and to present cooking demonstrations at health fairs at The Library of Congress, the Federal Judiciary Center, and the Department of Health and Human Services.

She also has performed cooking shows at various venues including the International Gourmet Show at the Capital Center, the Home and Design Show at the Washington Convention Center, the Chinese American Heritage Day at Alexandria Market Square, and many gourmet stores. In April 1999, she was invited to the Federal Reserve Board for a speaking engagement and cooking demonstration on the topic: "Food, Nutrition, Health and the Economy."

She has been featured in many newspapers and magazines, including *The Washington Post, The Baltimore Sun, The Montgomery Journal, The Sentinel, The Capital Hill Rag, Washingtonian, Travel and Leisure, Saturday Evening Post,* and *Newsweek.*

She recently retired from her position as a chemist at the National Institutes of Health, where she received the coveted NIH Scientific Merit Award. Since 1994, she has been honored as the Woman of the Year, and inducted into the Hall of Fame of International Business and Professional Women's Who's Who in Food Service by the American Biographical Institute. She has been listed in Who's Who in the World, Who's Who in America, Who's Who of Finance and Industry, Who's Who of American Women, 2000 Notable Women, and Who's Who in the East. She is a member of the American Chemical Society and the International Association of Culinary Professionals. She has two daughters, and lives and teaches in Silver Spring, Maryland.

Introduction

Cuisine is a form of art and part of the great heritage of China. Brush painting is also a traditional art of the Chinese. The images on the cover of this book show my wonderful family heritage and celebrate its achievements. The four scrolls are original brush paintings of the Four Seasons with poems by a famous artist honoring my grandfather, Shih Suei-Teng, for his accomplishments. He passed the Ch'ing Dynasty National Civil Service Examination and received the title of Distinguished Scholar. He was offered the governorship and awarded lands in Taiwan. I am very proud of both my great-grandfather and grandfather, who were scholars of China and governors in Taiwan. On the cover, I am wearing a gold medal for The Woman of The Year 2000 (for outstanding community service and professional achievement), selected from the International Who's Who of Professional and Business Women and awarded by the American Biographical Institute. By fulfilling my professional aspirations, I am honoring my ancestors' memory.

Raised in Taiwan, born into a family of the aristocracy, I acquired gourmet tastes in my early childhood. In Rukuan, the ancient capital of Taiwan during the Ch'ing Dynasty, our ancestral home was built like a Mandarin Court and had a large gourmet kitchen. The kitchen had a custom-made brick oven fitted for four restaurant-size 22-inch woks or steamers. Chinese New Year was the most important event, when my father's whole family would get together to celebrate. I remember the relatives arriving, with the wonderful fragrance of Steamed New Year's Cakes coming from the kitchen, and the chopping noises of cleavers keeping us children awake. On early New Year's Day, the best chef in town was hired to prepare the banquet in our family kitchen. I was attracted by the good smell of the food, and would stay in the kitchen to watch the chef's team chopping and cooking energetically. They called me the little doll, and gave me some samples to taste. All the dishes were so delicious and elaborately decorated. As I watched the chef carving vegetables and fruits into beautiful flowers, birds, and dragons, I wished that someday I could cook and carve just like him. My penchant for gourmet cooking is rooted in those early experiences.

The Chinese people are fond of their cuisine and take it seriously. The wide range and complexity of Chinese cuisine reflects the country's long history, economic development, geographical differences, social and cultural refinement, and creativity of the people. The foundation of *The Art of The Chinese Cookery* is based on the principle of Ying and Yang (cold and hot, mild and strong) in balance. Thus, a harmonious mixture of meat and vegetables in a dish is the desired result. There are five regional schools of Chinese cooking that have developed throughout the centuries: Canton, Fukien, Shantung, Szechuan, and Honan.

Besides the traditional Fukien (Eastern) School of Cooking, Taiwanese cooking features seafood. Sushi and Japanese cuisine are also very popular on the island. After I came to study in the United States, I found that among the things I missed most were fresh fish and the good home cooking of Taiwan. Until the 1970s, most supermarkets in the United States did not carry fresh fish. The only Chinese canned goods sold were chop suey and chow mein, and Chinese restaurants only served Cantonese food. After my daughters were born, I decided to teach Chinese cooking part time rather than going back to work full time as a chemist. I wanted to introduce Americans to the authentic, delicious, and healthful Chinese cuisine on which I had been raised.

In the summer of 1973, I studied Chinese cuisine at the Wei-Chuan Foods Corporation in Taipei, Taiwan, and graduated with a certificate. Upon my return to the United States, I was asked by the director of the Montgomery County public school system to design and teach the course, Chinese Cooking I, for their adult education program. It was over-whelmingly popular because during the 1970s Americans started focusing on diet, exercise, and natural foods. My recipes that used natural and lighter foods did satisfy these trends. My adult education students liked my teaching and recipes, and wanted further instruction, so I decided to open my own cooking school. In February of 1975, The Chinese Cookery was incorporated in the State of Maryland. Located at 1049-R Rockville Pike, Rockville, Maryland, my cooking school offered Chinese cooking instruction in three levels: Basic, Advanced, and Gourmet, as well as retail sales of utensils, food, and gifts.

In August 1975, shortly after my cooking school opened, I was interviewed by *Newsweek* magazine and written up in the article, "Food: The New Wave." I stated that the popularity of my cooking class was partly due to health concerns since in most Chinese cooking there is relatively little cholesterol (one pound of meat sliced and stir-fried with vegetables will serve four or five people). Another factor contributing to the popularity of my classes was the very personalized instruction I offered. Rather than the forty or more students I taught in each adult education class, I purposely limited the class size at my cooking school so that it would lend itself not only to demonstration, but also, to active participation. With the success of those classes, and to satisfy my students' appetite for additional classes, I added another level, Gourmet II, in 1978. This level featured more seafood dishes than Gourmet I, which focused on meats. By 1980, I had added two additional levels: Gourmet III, including more desserts and dishes that require special technique, and Szechuan, hot and spicy Chinese cuisine. Dim-sum, a popular form of Chinese appetizers, are included in the last two lessons of the three Gourmet levels.

After my daughters left home for college, I decided to remodel the lower level of my home and relocate my cooking school there. In 1986, upon approval by the zoning board and the issue of a new license, I set up a well-equipped cooking classroom in my house, with a custom-made Chinese brick oven on the patio. Since most of my students were interested in evening or weekend classes, I also decided to return to work as a full-time chemist at the National Institutes of Health (NIH). I continued to teach cooking classes in the evenings, and added a seventh level, Hunan. In 1990, when Americans started eating more fresh fish for good health, I set up a Japanese Sushi class. My students enjoyed par-ticipating in making professional quality Sushi—they were surprised at their ability to imitate Sushi chefs so effortlessly and proficiently!

Last year I retired from NIH in order to focus my efforts on running my cooking school and publishing this cookbook. This year I created another level, Vegetarian, which I started teaching in February. When I went back to Taiwan in 1993, I studied vegetarian cooking with the famous Chef Ho Wei-Shiung of the Buddhist Temple Restaurant. In my Vegetarian class I recreated classic recipes to appeal to American tastes while retaining recipe authenticity. Chinese vegetarian cuisine, which has a long history, is sophisticated and nutritionally abundant. The use of soy protein is absolutely essential.

In my class, I teach the procedure for making varieties of vegetarian meat-replacements called Vegetarian Fish, Vegetarian Steak, and Braised Yellow Partridge (a classic Chinese vegetarian dish). After making the vegetarian "meat," I cook it with other vegetables to make a nutritional dish. All the recipes are in this book. You will find them so delicious that you will change your mind about tofu!

I especially enjoy teaching Chinese cuisine, because I have been fortunate to have students who are very eager to learn. I am pleased that they find my recipes delicious and authentic and like the style of my personalized teaching. They are appreciative that I write recipes precisely, which is due in part to my chemistry training. It has been my good fortune that the knowledge of food ingredients obtained from my father, and the artistic presentation of the dishes inspired by my mother, have made my teaching continuously popular for all these years.

This book is organized exactly following my instruction at The Chinese Cookery School starting from Level I (Basic), progressing through Level II (Advanced), Levels III, IV, and V (Gourmet I, II, and III), Level VI (Szechuan), Level VII (Hunan), and Level VIII (Vegetarian). I encourage you to start with the dishes in Basic. This level contains some of the more popular Chinese stir-frying dishes that require simple technique and are easy to make.

The basic technique of cutting and the proper use of utensils, including the cleaver, turner, wok, and steamers, are very essential in mastering Chinese cooking. Working speed is also very important. As you try making the simpler recipes, you should focus on developing your skills in these fundamental areas. In the last two lessons of the Advanced Level and up the dishes are more difficult and take longer to prepare.

I have given a lot of thought and worked hard to produce a genuine Chinese gourmet taste in all of my recipes, which I think you will find much better than the ones served in Chinese restaurants. Using this book, you can cook authentic, nutritional Chinese dishes that will impress your family and friends.

Acknowledgements

To my parents, the late Dr. and Mrs. Luke Chian-Hsi Shih, who inspired and guided me to achieve my goal today, I express my love, respect, and gratitude. My father was a dedicated physician in Taiwan and also an exceptional father, showing great concern for his children's health and studies. Every night after finishing with his patients, he always checked my homework and spent a few minutes talking to me. Without my father's love and support, I would not be here and have my success today. He was always very proud of me and encouraged me to accomplish things on my own, like coming to study in the United States. Today, as my cookbook is published, my dream comes true. I wish he were here to share the honor which he equally deserves. This is my legacy for my daughters, grandchildren, and the generations to follow.

To my late husband, Kenneth Carducci, an expert in computer systems work, who helped me start up The Chinese Cookery, Inc., and worked tirelessly towards making my retail and cooking school business flourish, I express my wholehearted gratitude.

To my daughters, Suzanne and Elizabeth, who also have helped me in my cooking school activities, I thank you both. Today, Suzanne is a doctor of optometry, and Elizabeth, a marketing consultant with a B.S. degree in Electrical Engineering from MIT and an MBA from Stanford University. To my daughter, Elizabeth, and her husband, Chris, who have helped me in the self-publishing of my cookbook, I say many thanks or Tuo-Shieh in Chinese. Elizabeth who has experience in international marketing, Suzanne, and her husband, David, will be working together in the marketing of this book. I thank you in advance for your efforts.

To Favorite Recipes Press (FRP), especially Debbi Booten, Jim Scott, and Georgia Brazil, I thank you for your cooperation and fine job in the production of my cookbook. I would also like to thank Melvin Bergman, my friend and student, for his sound legal advice on this project.

Finally, to all my students and graduates who have shown a great interest in my classes and exhibited enthusiastic support for my work over the past twenty-eight years, I thank you for your business. You have made my teaching rewarding, and the publication of this book possible!

The Art of Chinese Cookery

The Chinese emphasize good eating. Lin Yu-Tang declares that if there is anything the Chinese are serious about, it is food. Confucius, a passionate gourmet, taught that good taste in food was to be cultivated as a part of artistic living.

Chinese philosophy and art depend on harmony. Chinese cuisine is an art: It is the art of mixture based on the principle of Taoism, Yin-Yang (cold and hot, mild and strong, vegetables and meat) in balance. Confucianism advocates harmony, thus the harmonious mixture in dishes is desired.

Great importance is also given to texture in addition to aroma, visual appeal, and taste. Texture is very important in stir-fried dishes where the texture of vegetables should be crispy and crunchy, while the meat should be tender. If vegetables are over-cooked, the dish will not only lose the crispy texture but also some of its nutritional value.

Preparation of Chinese food takes great care and, in most cases, a longer time than does the actual cooking. Preparation in Chinese cooking, for the most part, refers to cutting. There are always two chefs in a Chinese restaurant, one chef cutting and the other cooking. If the mixture of foods, meat and vegetables, are not cut into the same size, the foods will not finish cooking at the same time.

The technique of cutting both for size and shape is of prime importance. Different ingredients blend into surprising harmony when cut to uniform size and perhaps even more importantly, to correct shape, for the shape determines the cooking area. Cooking time is short, only two minutes with high heat for stir-frying. So, all the prepared foods, seasonings, and mixes must be placed within reach of the stove.

There is no main course in a Chinese meal, for there is interest in variety. A large banquet may consist of as many as ten to twenty dishes.

Five Schools of Chinese Cuisine

China is a big land. From North to South and East to West the weather changes greatly, thus the food products vary by the regions. The Chinese are economical. For centuries they have depended on local products for survival and have developed distinct types of cuisine using suitable methods of cooking. In general, five schools of Chinese cuisine have evolved.

The Canton School (Southern)

The Canton School (Southern) is the best known outside of China. Throughout the year, a wide variety of fruits and vegetables are available. The Cantonese invented the stir-frying method, so vegetables are not over-cooked.

Other methods, such as roasting and grilling, also originated here. Traditionally, marinated meats such as spareribs, chicken, and duck were hung and barbecued over a charcoal fire. (The special marinating sauce is Hoisin Sauce.) Now Chinese restaurants have adapted the hanging method for barbecue in the oven so meats are cooked very lean.

Rice is the main crop and steamed rice is served at every meal. Ginger and scallion are used for seasoning. Dim-sum (which means Little Heart-Delights in Chinese) is popularly served for lunch in Cantonese restaurants.

The Fukien School (Eastern)

The Fukien School (Eastern) is known for incorporating all types of Chinese cooking. This geographic area is located along the Pacific coast and along the Yangtze River. The climate is sub-tropical, and the food products are abundant throughout the year.

Many wealthy Chinese live here, with the result that family cooks and restaurant chefs come from all parts of China and have introduced different styles of Chinese cooking. This cuisine is cosmopolitan and sophisticated.

The Fukienese invented Clear Steamed Soup Stock (page 28). Fish dishes are featured, and steamed rice is served with each meal. Ginger and green onion are the main seasonings.

The Shantung School (Northern)

The Shantung School (Northern) is the origin of Peking cuisine. Because of the long, cold winter, it is characterized by cooking or steaming in wine sauce. The major product is wheat and the staple foods are buns, dumplings, and noodles made of wheat flour.

Garlic and leek are the seasonings; bean sauce, providing more protein, is the main condiment; and rice vinegar is used in dipping sauce. Peking Duck (page 106) is the most celebrated banquet dish.

The Szechuan School (Western)

The Szechuan School (Western) is characterized by very hot and spicy food in response to the humid summer months. Often four or five kinds of chile peppers are used in a dish in the belief that it will help the eater perspire, while spices help breathing. Hot Bean Sauce, soy paste with generous amounts of chiles, is the key flavoring to the hot taste in Szechuan dishes.

Szechuan, a great mountain-ranged basin, and neighboring provinces are covered with snow in winter. Fresh vegetables harvested during the summer months are sun-dried or pickled as preserves. The taste of this cuisine is complex with the use of dried vegetables and vinegar to help digestion. An example is Hot and Sour Soup (page 54).

The Honan School (Central North)

The Honan School (Central North), not to be confused with Hunan cuisine which resembles the hot and spicy Szechuan School, originated sweet and sour dishes. Sour indicates vinegar which helps in the digestion of wheat gluten, and sweet is from sugar to give a balancing taste. The best known original dish is Sweet and Sour Pork (page 30). The use of garlic dominates the taste of the cuisine.

Honan Province is located south of the Yellow River. It is geographically classified as a part of northern China.

Fundamental Methods of Chinese Cooking

Stir-Frying

Stir-Frying is characterized by a rapid circular stirring motion using a Chinese turner over high heat throughout 2 to 3 minutes of frying time. Add 2 tablespoons vegetable oil each time after the wok is heated. Since the cooking time is very short and frying is rapid, the food is not over-cooked and will maintain the original texture and nutritional value.

All the ingredients that go into the same wok must be sliced very uniformly thin and diagonally to create the larger cooking area exposed to the heat. Cutting in this manner is called match-stick julienne. The stir-fry method of cooking is especially great for fresh vegetables.

Red Cooking

Red Cooking is also referred to as the braised method or stewing. This method is wonderful for cooking meats which are cut into 1½-inch cubes. The chicken can be cut through the bone into cubes with a cleaver. The red color comes from the color of soy sauce.

This method has a precise technique: First add 2 tablespoons oil to a hot wok and stir-fry green onion, ginger, and the meats. Then add soy sauce, honey, wine, water, and ½ teaspoon Chinese five-spice powder.

Next turn the heat down from high to medium-low and cover the wok. Continue cooking for 25 minutes. This method of long simmering results in very tender, flavorful meats and rich red, thick juice for flavoring steamed rice.

Deep-Frying

Deep-Frying requires the use of frying oil which can be heated to the temperature of 350 degrees without smoking and maintain that temperature even after the cold pieces of meat, seafood, fruit, and vegetable are added. Only two, peanut and soybean oil, can do the job.

The amount of oil is important. For a 14-inch wok, 6 cups peanut or soybean oil is required (4 cups of oil for a 12-inch wok). When finished frying, let the oil cool down completely, then skim and save in a dark bottle or can. Reuse for deep-frying only.

Steaming

Steaming is the most healthful way of cooking. Nothing is added and only the rising steam cooks the food, thus producing the most natural and sweet tastes. The boiling water is not touching the food as the very hot steam rises through the holes of the steam plate. The steam plate placed inside the wok is lightly oiled with the food on the top and the steamer is tightly covered.

There are different varieties of steamers. Chinese bamboo steamers can be fitted with several steamer baskets that stack and steam many dim-sum or other different dishes all at the same time. The steamer set is certainly an efficient energy saving cooking utensil.

Roasting

Roasting in Chinese cooking is the same as barbecue in the traditional way. The meats, ribs, even a whole suckling pig, ducks, or chicken are first marinated in Chinese barbecue sauce (Hoisin Sauce), wine, honey, soy sauce, garlic, ginger, and green onion, then hung on a bamboo rod over a charcoal fire.

While cooking, baste every 15 minutes. The fat will drip down, and the meats will be roasted lean and crispy.

Utensils

The basic Chinese utensils are the wok, the turner (Chinese spatula), the ladle, the mesh-wire strainer, the Chinese cleaver, the steam plate, the steamer set, the Mongolian Fire Pot, the Genghis Khan Barbecue Pan, the Yunnan Steam Pot, and a supply of cooking chopsticks.

Wok: The Function

A wok is the major cooking utensil in China. It is very versatile and can be used for different methods of cooking. It is especially suitable for stir-frying because of its somewhat conical shape, with a wide, round opening at the top and the gradually sloping sides, which makes foods spin inside when turning with a spatula. The foods do not sit at the bottom and can be mixed evenly without burning when cooked on high heat. The shape of the wok also reduces evaporation of liquid, so less oil or water is needed for cooking.

Wok: The Materials

Woks can be made of different kinds of metal:
- Steel—Steel is a good conductor of heat. A heavy-gauge steel wok is the best for its functionality and price. It conducts heat quickly and retains it evenly. The old-fashioned wok is made of steel or iron.
- Aluminum—Aluminum conducts heat quickly but unevenly, and cools down faster than steel.
- Stainless Steel with Copper-Clad Bottom—Stainless steel is not good in conducting heat, but copper is. Wok cooking is known for rapid cooking with high heat, so it is advisable to buy any stainless steel wok with a copper-clad bottom.
- Non-Stick—Non-stick finishes on woks have been improved in recent years. Be sure to use only a wooden spatula for stir-frying. The advantage of a non-stick wok is that you can use water instead of oil for stir-frying; therefore, it is recommended for someone avoiding oil intake.
- Electric—An electric wok is nice for entertaining at the table, but the heat is not responsive instantly and may not reach the indicated higher temperatures.

Wok: The Shapes

Even with variations, the wide opening and sloping sides remain.
- Flat-Bottom is good for use with an electric stove because the bottom sits flat on the burner for direct contact with the heat.
- Round-Bottom is fine for use with either gas or electric stoves. Remove the wok from its stand to place directly on the burner.
- Two-Handle is easy to move from the burner while full.
- Long Wood Handle is especially useful for stir-frying. Hold onto the handle to move the wok away when the heat is too high, and mix the foods in the air by flipping the wok in lieu of stirring. A second handle opposite the long handle makes for easy lifting.

Season an Iron or Steel Wok Before Use

A drop of water will rust the surface of a steel or iron wok. Remove the spot with a bit of cleanser and water on a Teflon sponge pad. Rinse with hot water and towel dry completely.

Since an iron or steel wok will rust, it is important to "season" the wok before its first use. To season the wok, pour 1 tablespoon of vegetable oil onto a paper towel and wipe the entire inner area of the wok. Place the wok on the stove over very low heat for eight minutes to bond a thin-layer of oil coating to the surface of the wok. Now the wok is clean and ready for cooking!

Do not clean the wok in a dishwasher or the seasoning protection will be lost and the above procedure must be repeated.

Turner (Chinese Spatula)

It is essential to have a Turner (Chinese Spatula) which differs from a regular spatula. There are three important features in this utensil to facilitate stir-frying: the sides are slightly turned up, the blade and corners are curved to slide easily over the curves of a wok, and the metal handle is very stiff.

Ladle

Ladle is the same as any regular ladle for serving soup.

Mesh-Wire Strainer

Mesh-Wire Strainer is an important utensil for deep-frying. The bamboo handle stays cool while you are holding and deep-frying. The strainer is made of mesh-wire, and can be used for easy straining and pressing gently to test for doneness. It is made of brass and comes in different sizes, but the 6-inch diameter size is the most popular to buy and use.

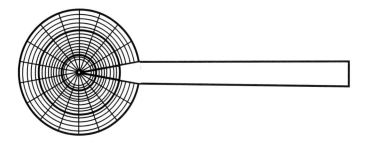

Chinese Cleaver

Chinese Cleaver is the most important cutting tool for Chinese cooking preparation. You should buy a good all-purpose cleaver which can be used to cut, slice, mince, tenderize, and transport. The blade should be very sharp for cutting, chopping the bones, and slicing into thin pieces. Mash and bruise garlic cloves by pressing with the flat side of the blade to remove the skins and then mince. Crush peppercorns using the back of the wooden handle. The blade size is designated by number. The all-purpose size is #1 through #3 and is made of steel or stainless steel. Carbon steel is refined steel and the blade can be chipped when cutting through bones. The numbers represent the size and weight of the cleaver with the smaller numbers designating the larger, heavier cleavers. Those numbered 4 and up refer to slicers only, and are not meant to be used for chopping.

Steam Plate

Steam Plate for steaming is made of aluminum or stainless steel. It is round and perforated with uniform holes. The 10-inch diameter is for a 12-inch wok and the 12-inch size is for a 14-inch family-size wok. The steam plate fits into a wok 1-inch down from the top edge. Lightly oil the plate before placing the food on the top. The wok should be filled with water one-third full and covered with the lid for steaming.

Steamer Set

The classic Steamer Set is made of bamboo and is made up of several stacking baskets with the cover. This steamer is the best energy-saving utensil. The steam is hot and completely entrapped within the steamer as the steam rises to the lid, cooking food in the entire stack at the same time. This method of cooking is very popular in the north and also for making Dim-sum.

Make sure to lightly oil the top of each stack, or place a piece of moistened and oiled cheesecloth in each basket, before placing the food for steaming. It is very practical for steaming several dishes. Place the food that needs the longest cooking time at the bottom and foods with lesser cooking times on top. For example: Place Chiao-Tzu (meat dumplings, page 44) on the bottom for 25 minutes, potato slices in the middle for 15 minutes, and thin pancakes for 10 minutes on the top. Set the timer. Upon ringing, remove the top stack, then the middle and the bottom last.

To care for and maintain a bamboo steamer: After washing with very hot water, hang to air-dry. Do not soak the bamboo steamer in water, the shape will be warped so that the baskets will no longer stack well.

Mongolian Fire Pot

Mongolian Fire Pot is a large vessel with a central chimney into which glowing charcoal is placed to cook the ingredients. The origin of unique fire-pot cooking began in Northern China, where the winters are bitterly cold. Food can be cooked and served hot at the table for a banquet or a big family gathering.

Soup stock is poured into the base of the vessel to fill and then heated. Very thin sliced meat and vegetables are added to the boiling soup for three to five minutes. Remove the lid, use a strainer to remove the meats and vegetables, and serve with a variety of sauces. Add preboiled noodles to the soup to make a complete meal. Fire-pot cooking is a healthful fondue-cooking method.

Genghis Khan Barbecue Pan

Genghis Khan Barbecue Pan is an inverted cast iron pan constructed to resemble the iron battle helmet of Genghis Khan's infantry.

The design of the pan is so unique that very little fuel is needed. The holes on the top throughout the dome are for the smoke to come through. The ridges and channels that are cast into the pan allow fat and juices to drain from the meats during cooking. A shallow lip at the bottom is the reservoir where the dripping juices collect.

This is a very healthful cooking method which can be used indoor on the stovetop or outdoor on a hibachi grill. Fresh foods are sliced very thin, meats are marinated before placing on the pan for rapid grilling, and everything is served hot with a variety of dipping sauces.

Yunnan Steam Pot

Yunnan Steam Pot is a lidded earthenware casserole with a pointed chimney rising through the center of the pot and almost reaching to the lid for even distribution of steam. It is a unique steamer suitable for cooking in high altitude areas like Yunnan Province.

Water is not directly added to the meat, but the condensation of vapor will cook the meat moist and tender, and accumulate into rich broth at the bottom of the pot.

Cooking Chopsticks

Cooking Chopsticks are useful mixing and cooking tools. The ends are pointed for easier mixing or dripping the beaten egg through the sticks in making the fine, soft shreds in Egg Drop Soup (page 28).

Cooking chopsticks are long which makes them safe and suitable for holding food while deep-frying.

Cutting Techniques

"Cutting" is "Preparing" in Chinese cooking. It is just as important as the actual cooking and requires even more time. Chinese cuisine is a form of art and science combined. The end product is a well-balanced, nutritional dish with a mixture of different ingredients cooked in harmony.

Because the cooking method uses high heat and is rapid, all the ingredients are cut into a uniform size and shape in order to finish cooking in two to three minutes. The technique of cutting into shapes is integral to the method of cooking and consists of the following basic cuts:

Shred or Julienne

Shred or Julienne is the term used for the cutting of meats and vegetables into very thin diagonal shreds resembling matchsticks. Cutting meat across the grain makes the meat less chewy. Vegetables sliced diagonally create a larger area exposed to heat for faster cooking. Shreds are suitable for stir-fry.

Cube

Cube meats, including chicken cut through bones, into uniform cubes about $1^1/2$ inches. Cubed meats are best for steaming, braising and stewing.

Dice

Dice foods by cutting them into small cubes (called ding in Chinese). Diced foods are good for stir-frying. Big thin dices are used for deep-frying.

Rolling-Cut Cubes

Rolling-Cut Cubes result when using a special skill which is difficult to describe but simple when demonstrated. To roll down a carrot, roll the carrot 45 degrees ($1/8$ of a turn) each time toward the chopping board before making each cut and cut into cubes. These cubes cut with angles are excellent for stewing.

Mince

Mince or finely chop is for strong-flavored ingredients, such as garlic and ginger, which should be peeled and minced before dropping into the oil for stir-fry dishes.

Ingredients

At The Chinese Cookery, Inc., students attending classes may purchase Chinese and Japanese food products for practicing the dishes at home. This section lists basic ingredients used in this, as well as other chapters. Additional ingredients for making Szechuan and Hunan regional cuisines, or specialty foods such as Vegetarian, are described in those chapters. Most of these ingredients may be purchased at Asian food markets.

Bean Sprouts

Bean Sprouts are light and nutritious vegetables, and very popular for use in salads or stir-fry dishes because of their crunchy texture. Fresh sprouts of mung beans (or green beans), may be purchased in the vegetable sections of many large grocery stores.

Bean sprouts may also be sprouted at home from purchased mung beans using the following method:

1. Soak the green beans overnight in warm water.
2. Prepare a foil pan by puncturing many holes in the bottom and lining the bottom with cheesecloth. The cheesecloth will allow the bean roots to grow through the holes and support the bean sprouts to stand as they grow.
3. Spread the soaked beans evenly over the cheesecloth and cover lightly with a heavy cloth, such as a blanket. Place in a dark, warm place.
4. Sprinkle water over the beans every six to eight hours.
5. After four days the sprouts will have grown to about 2 inches, and will be ready to eat or use for cooking.

Bean Threads or Bean Noodles (Fensi)

Bean Threads or Bean Noodles (Fensi) are made of mung bean starch and water. They are good for use in soups, as in Szechuan Cabbage, Pork and Bean Thread Soup (page 64), or deep-fried to make puffed bean threads as in Dragon Phoenix Paradise (page 100).

Thicker bean threads can be boiled briefly, drained, rinsed with cold water, and served cold with shreds of meat and fresh vegetables as in Assorted Three-Shreds Cold Plate (page 62).

Chili Oil (Sesame Chili Oil)

Chili Oil (Sesame Chili Oil) is called red oil in Chinese. There are two kinds of chili oil, one with a cotton seed base and one with a sesame seed base.

Sesame Chili Oil, which is sesame oil with red chili peppers, is more flavorful and recommended for use in recipes in this book. It is the most important flavoring and garnish in Szechuan and Hunan Cuisine, imparting the fragrance of sesame oil plus plenty of hot taste to the dishes.

Coriander

Coriander is also called cilantro or Chinese parsley. Coriander gives a more unique aroma and flavor to Chinese cooking than regular parsley. Do not chop the leaves.

Dried Black Mushrooms (Shiitake)

Dried Black Mushrooms, also called Shiitake Mushrooms in Japanese, are the dried black mushrooms that grow on a certain oak tree called Shii.

Chinese and Japanese have long recognized the advantages of this mushroom with its anti-cancer elements for health and its unique fragrance for cooking.

Fresh Shiitake Mushrooms can now be purchased in many stores. Until recently only imported dried shiitake mushrooms were available.

To prepare for cooking, soak dried mushrooms in boiling water for 15 minutes. When they are soft, squeeze the excess water out, trim the stems and slice the caps into shreds for stir-frying.

Dried Shrimp

Dried Shrimp are dehydrated shrimp with an exotic aroma. They are great for cooking with meat in dishes like Traditional Chinese Tamales (page 84) or Dry-Fried String Beans (page 131).

Duck Sauce

Duck Sauce is also called golden plum sauce. Duck Sauce is used as a dipping sauce for Egg Rolls (page 34) and Fried Wontons (page 33). It is less tangy than plum sauce because there are not whole pieces of ginger in this sauce.

Egg Noodles

Egg Noodles are thin, round, long strands made of egg, wheat flour and water (see Chinese Fresh Noodles, page 98). Making fresh noodles by hand is an ancient Chinese culinary art; however, you can now use a pasta machine to produce similar results.

Fresh and dried noodles are sold commercially. Dried noodles have a longer shelf-life; fresh noodles should be kept in the freezer if storing for longer than one week. Use Egg Noodles for making lo-mein (stir-fried with vegetables and sauce) or noodle soup.

Egg Roll Wrappers

Egg Roll Wrappers are made of egg, flour, and water and are packaged and sold commercially either refrigerated or frozen. If stored in the freezer, the Wrappers (or skins) must be thawed in the refrigerator overnight or at room temperature for two hours before making Egg Rolls (page 34).

Five-Spice Powder

Five-Spice Powder is a ground powder containing five spices: Chinese fennel, cinnamon, clove, nutmeg, and star anise. It is a great seasoning for cooking red meats. The meat can be served cold, as in a dish called Five-Fragrant Pork (or Beef), or hot with the very rich juice used as a gravy for Steamed White Rice (page 26).

Green Onion

Green Onion is also called spring onion or scallion and is an important flavoring agent in Chinese cooking. To use, trim both ends of the scallion and cut the white, firm part into 1/4-inch dices. The green part is sliced into 1/8-inch pieces. Separate the white and green parts. Use the white part when stir-frying to flavor the oil, and the green part as a garnish before serving.

Hoisin Sauce

Hoisin Sauce is a thick, sweet, and pungent Cantonese barbecue sauce. It is made from soybean paste, sugar, salt, vinegar, garlic, spices, cornstarch, chili, and sesame oil. It is a key flavoring in the marinade for barbecue and also used as a dipping sauce or spread for thin pancakes. Keep in the refrigerator until ready to use.

Oyster Sauce

Oyster Sauce is thick, brown, and richly flavored. It originated in Canton and is made from extract of oysters combined with soy sauce, molasses, and cornstarch. It is a classic sauce used to make Beef in Oyster Sauce (page 50).

Peanut Oil

Peanut Oil is used especially in deep-frying because peanut oil retains high temperatures up to 400 degrees F without smoking. The average deep-frying temperature is 350 degrees F. Using peanut oil results in shorter deep-frying time and crisper food.

Plum Sauce

Plum Sauce is a sweet and tart dipping sauce for Barbecue Roast Pork (page 41) or duck. Plum sauce is made from boiling together the extracted juice of ripe plums with water, salt, sugar, vinegar, ginger, spices, and cornstarch.

Rice

Rice for making Chinese steamed rice or fried rice is long grain white rice. It is preferred because of its cooked texture which is relatively dry and easily separated. The best kind is the fragrant, Jasmine long grain rice from Thailand.

Rice Noodles

Rice Noodles are made from rice and water. The dried, long strands made commercially are called rice sticks. The best kind, *Shin-Chu Rice Noodle* (Bi-Fen), is a product of Taiwan. To use, soak the noodles in cold water first, then stir-fry with meat, shrimp, vegetables and sauce.

Rice Vinegar

Rice Vinegar is genuinely brewed from rice and tastes mild and smooth compared to other vinegars. It is the most important condiment for making sushi and sweet and sour dishes.

Use the regular, unsweetened kind for cooking in dishes such as Sweet and Sour Pork (page 30), Hot and Sour Soup (page 54), and Japanese Sushi (page 102). Gourmet rice vinegar, which is flavored with sugar, is excellent for use in salad dressings.

Sesame Oil

Sesame Oil is a fragrant oil made from roasted sesame seeds.

Soy Sauce

Soy Sauce is the most important seasoning in oriental cooking. It is made from fermented soybeans mixed with crushed wheat, salt, sugar, and water. (See Vegetarian Chapter—Soybeans). There are three different types of soy sauce:

All-purpose Soy Sauce or *Dark Soy Sauce* is made from yellow-brown soybeans. This soy sauce looks darker and is used in cooking pork or beef dishes.

Light-Colored Soy Sauce is called Usuguchi Shoyu in Japanese or Thin Soy in Chinese. This sauce is made from white soybeans which are rarer and imported from Japan. It looks thinner and light in color, so it is used in cooking fish, seafood, chicken, and turkey dishes.

Lite Soy Sauce is Dark Soy Sauce with 40 percent of the salt content removed; therefore, it is good for those restricting their salt intake. To maintain a full flavor, use this sauce in the latter stages of cooking for garnishing soups, braising sauce, stir-frying dishes, or as a dipping sauce.

Sweet Rice (Glutinous Rice)

Sweet Rice (Glutinous Rice) is used for making New Year's Cake, sticky rice, Eight-Jewels Rice Pudding (page 89), and other Dim-sums. The grain is short, round, slightly sweet, and glutinous, and is suitable for making desserts.

Sweet Rice Cooking Wine

Sweet Rice Cooking Wine is made from sweet rice (glutinous rice). The Japanese call this seasoning Aji-Mirin. It is an ingredient in the marinade for Teriyaki sauce. It imparts a wine flavor to the food, as well as tenderizing the meat in the dish.

Use this wine whenever a recipe calls for pale dry sherry. Keep the wine at room temperature.

Wonton Wrappers

Wonton Wrappers (or skins) are only a quarter of the size of egg roll wrappers, and are used for making wontons. Similar to egg roll wrappers, packages of 45 wonton skins may be purchased refrigerated or frozen, but must be thawed prior to use.

Tea

Hot Tea is the most important drink to the Chinese. My father, a medical doctor and tea connoisseur, often said that tea can cure fatigue, lift one's spirit, help digestion, and regulate body temperature. These comments have also been recorded from the books of tea master, Lu Yu, and Taoists.

There are three categories of tea: unfermented, semi-fermented, and fermented tea. Fermentation occurs during the drying process. The longer the drying period, the more fermented the tea becomes, thus producing a stronger taste and darker color.

Unfermented Tea

Green Tea, the most pure and medicinal tea, is light in color and has a delicate taste. The Chinese drink green tea in the morning because it helps remove toxic substances from the intestinal tract. Green Tea is believed to have anti-oxidant and anti-cancer effects. There are several kinds of green tea: Gunpowder, Dragon Well, and Pouchong.

Jasmine Tea is known for the fragrance of jasmine, and is light in color.

Semi-Fermented Tea

Oolong Tea is orange in color and has a rich, wonderful taste. Some blends are mixed with ginseng to give energy and vitality. Oolong Tea is a good accompaniment to banquet dishes. Taiwan produces the best Oolong (Black Dragon) tea, including Tien-Wu (Sky Mist) and Tung-Ting.

Chinese Restaurant Tea is a well-known variety, which is a mixture of Oolong and black tea.

Fermented Tea

Yunnan Tea is the best example of fermented tea, or black tea. Yunnan Tea is dark in color and strong in taste.

Steamed White Rice

Ingredients:

2 cups uncooked extra-long grain rice
(Jasmine rice)
3 cups cold water

Procedure:

(Note: When preparing rice for only two people, reduce the amounts to 1½ cups rice and 2½ cups cold water to yield 4 cups cooked rice.)

1. Combine the rice and the water in saucepan. Bring to a boil over high heat and cook, uncovered, for about 10 minutes or until "fish eyes" (tiny craters) form over the surface.

2. Cover the pan and reduce the heat to very low. Simmer for about 5 minutes. Remove from the heat, keep covered, and set aside until ready to serve.

YIELD: *4 servings.* **Nutritional Facts Per Serving:** Calories 140; Total Fat 0g (Saturated Fat 0g); Cholesterol 0mg; Sodium 0mg; Total Carbohydrate 31g (Dietary Fiber 1g, Sugars 0g); Protein 3g

Learn to hold the chopsticks correctly. Once you have mastered the correct technique, practice each time you eat a Chinese meal. Chinese children begin practicing the art of using chopsticks from the age of three using small chopsticks suitable for their small hands.

Chopsticks are made to taper from heavier at one end to more slender at the other.

Mastering Chopsticks

1. Place one of the chopsticks across the palm of the hand at the base of the fingers with the heavier end of the chopstick lying between the index finger and the thumb with about one-third of the length of the chopstick extending beyond the index finger. Fold the thumb to grasp the chopstick tightly as this chopstick should remain stationary while eating. Fold the little finger and ring finger into the palm under the chopstick.

2. Place the second chopstick between the thumb and index finger between the base and tips of the fingers in a manner similar to a pencil to allow the second chopstick to move. Allow the middle finger to touch the bottom chopstick lightly (figure 1).

3. Practice moving the second (upper) chopstick in a motion that permits the tips of the chopsticks to separate and move together in a scissoring motion that will permit picking up the small pieces of food from the dish and holding securely while bringing the food to the mouth (figure 2).

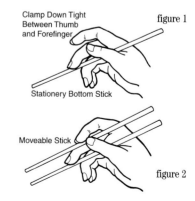

Clamp Down Tight
Between Thumb
and Forefinger

figure 1

Stationery Bottom Stick

Moveable Stick

figure 2

Shredded Beef with Green Pepper (Pepper Steak Canton) *(photo: page 65)*

Ingredients:

1 pound flank steak or beef top round
1/4 cup soy sauce
2 tablespoons rice wine or pale dry sherry
2 tablespoons cornstarch
2 teaspoons sugar
1 teaspoon salt
3 green bell peppers
2 green onions
1/4 cup vegetable oil
Pinch of salt
2 slices fresh gingerroot, minced

Preparation:

- Cut the steak into strips about 1 1/2 inches in length and 1/3 inch thick. Place the strips in a bowl.
- Combine the soy sauce, rice wine, cornstarch, sugar and 1 teaspoon salt in a small bowl and mix until the cornstarch, sugar and salt are completely dissolved. Pour the mixture over the steak strips and mix until coated. Marinate for 10 minutes.
- Cut the green peppers into fourths and remove and discard the seeds and membranes. Cut the green peppers diagonally into thin 1 1/2-inch-long shreds and set aside.
- Discard the green onion tops and cut the white portions into 1/4-inch dice.

Procedure:

1. Heat the wok over high heat. Add 2 tablespoons of the oil and the pinch of salt. Add the green peppers and stir-fry for about 1 minute or until tender-crisp. Remove the peppers and set aside.

2. Heat the wok over high heat. Add the remaining 2 tablespoons of the oil, the green onions and the gingerroot. Stir-fry until fragrant.

3. Add the steak and stir-fry for about 20 seconds or until the red color begins to disappear. Return the green peppers to the wok and stir-fry for several seconds longer until the steak is no longer red and the mixture is well mixed. Serve immediately.

YIELD: *5 servings.* **Nutritional Facts Per Serving:** Calories 250; Total Fat 15g (Saturated Fat 4g); Cholesterol 45 mg; Sodium 790 mg; Total Carbohydrate 8g (Dietary Fiber 1g, Sugars 2g), Protein 20g

Egg Drop Soup *(photo: page 65)*

Ingredients:

1 scallion
2 tablespoons cornstarch
¼ cup cold water
2 eggs
4 cups Clear Steamed Soup Stock
(see below)
Pepper to taste
2 teaspoons sesame oil

Preparation:

- Rinse the scallion, cut into very fine ⅛-inch dice and set aside.
- Dissolve the cornstarch in the cold water in a small bowl and set aside.
- Beat the eggs thoroughly in a small bowl and set aside.
- Measure the Clear Steamed Soup Stock into a wok.

Procedure:

1. Bring the Soup Stock to a boil. Add the cornstarch mixture gradually, stirring constantly and cook until thickened, stirring constantly with a pair of cooking chopsticks.
2. Holding and moving the chopsticks in circles above the soup, let the beaten eggs drop through the chopsticks. This will take only about 3 seconds. Stir the soup and turn off the heat immediately.
3. Add the finely diced scallion, pepper and sesame oil and serve immediately.

The original title is Egg Blossom Soup. Cantonese restaurants changed the title to describe the technique that achieves the soft, flowery look of the eggs floating on the surface of the soup.

Clear Steamed Soup Stock

Ingredients:

2 whole chicken breasts and wings
4½ cups cold water
4 slices fresh gingerroot, minced
1 green onion
2 teaspoons salt

Preparation:

- Cut the chicken breast and wing meat from the bones. Reserve the meat for making Chicken with Cashew Nuts (page 29).

Procedure:

1. Place the bones and skin in a 2- to 3-quart saucepan to use in preparing the Soup Stock.
2. Add the cold water to the chicken skin and bones. Add the gingerroot and the green onion cut into 2-inch pieces. Add the salt.
3. Cover the saucepan and place over high heat. Cook for exactly 10 minutes; the mixture should have come to a boil.
4. Rearrange the chicken bones, replace the cover and reduce the heat to medium-low.
5. Remove the stock from the heat; the result should be a very rich stock. Skim the stock, discard the bones and skin and strain the stock.

YIELD: *5 servings.* **Nutritional Facts Per Serving:** Calories 80; Total Fat 5g (Saturated Fat 1g); Cholesterol 95mg; Sodium 380mg; Total Carbohydrate 4g (Dietary Fiber 0g, Sugars 0g); Protein 5g

Chicken with Cashew Nuts *(photo: page 65)*

Ingredients:

2 whole boneless skinless
   chicken breasts
2 tablespoons Hoisin sauce
1 tablespoon light soy sauce
1 tablespoon rice wine or pale
   dry sherry
1 tablespoon cornstarch
$1/8$ teaspoon pepper
2 scallions
4 tablespoons peanut oil
1 cup cashew nuts, blanched peanuts
   or walnuts

Preparation:

- Cut the chicken breasts into
  $1/4 \times 1/2 \times 3/4$-inch strips and place
  in a bowl.
- Combine the Hoisin sauce, light soy
  sauce, rice wine, cornstarch and
  pepper in a small bowl and mix until
  the cornstarch is completely dissolved.
  Pour the mixture over the chicken,
  mix well and set aside.
- Discard the green scallion tops, cut
  the whites into $1/4$-inch pieces and
  set aside.

Procedure:

1. Heat the wok, add the peanut oil and
   heat. Add the scallions and stir-fry
   until slightly brown and fragrant.
2. Add the chicken mixture and stir-fry
   over medium heat for 2 minutes or
   until the chicken is opaque.
3. Add the cashews and mix well.
   Serve immediately.

YIELD: *4 servings.* **Nutritional Facts Per Serving:** 380 Calories; Total Fat 27g (Saturated Fat 5g);
Cholesterol 25mg; Sodium 450mg; Total Carbohydrate 19g (Dietary Fiber 1g, Sugars 5g); Protein 18g

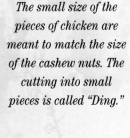

*The small size of the
pieces of chicken are
meant to match the size
of the cashew nuts. The
cutting into small
pieces is called "Ding."*

29

Sweet and Sour Pork (Hunan) *(photo: page 65)*

Use peanut or soybean oil for deep-frying. The average temperature of the oil for deep-frying is 350 degrees F. Only peanut or soybean oil can be heated to 350 degrees without smoking.

Use canola or other vegetable oil for stir-frying, if making a lighter dish.

Ingredients:

1 pound boneless pork loin

Batter:

1 egg
1/2 cup flour
1/2 teaspoon salt
1/3 cup water

1 or 2 green bell peppers
1 cup pineapple cubes

Sweet and Sour Sauce:

1/4 cup rice vinegar
1/4 cup water
1/4 cup sugar
1/4 cup ketchup
1/3 teaspoon salt
1 teaspoon soy sauce
2 teaspoons cornstarch

6 cups (about) oil for deep frying
2 tablespoons vegetable, peanut or
    corn oil
Pinch of salt
1/2 teaspoon minced garlic

Preparation:

- Cut the pork loin into 3/4-inch cubes, pound with the back of the cleaver and set aside.
- Prepare the Batter by beating the egg in a medium bowl. Add the flour, 1/2 teaspoon salt and water, mix until smooth. Mix in the pork cubes and set aside.
- Discard the seeds and membranes from the green peppers, cut the peppers into bite-size squares and set aside.
- Drain the pineapple cubes well and set aside.
- Prepare the Sweet and Sour Sauce ingredients by combining the rice vinegar, water, sugar, ketchup, salt, soy sauce and cornstarch in a small bowl, mix well and set aside.

Procedure:

1. Heat the 6 cups oil in a heavy pan such as a wok or deep fryer to 350 degrees. Add the batter-covered pork cubes, several pieces at a time, to the hot oil. Deep-fry for 3 minutes or until golden brown and remove to drain on paper towels. Set the deep-fried pork aside. Set the oil aside to cool.

2. Heat the wok over high heat. Add the 2 tablespoons oil, pinch of salt and the garlic. Stir-fry until fragrant. Add the green peppers and stir-fry for several seconds.

3. Add the pineapple and the Sweet and Sour Sauce and cook until well mixed and slightly thickend, stirring constantly.

4. Add the deep-fried pork when the sauce comes to a boil, mix lightly and serve immediately.

YIELD: *5 servings.* **Nutritional Facts Per Serving:** Calories 250; Total Fat 11g (Saturated Fat 2.5g); Cholesterol 75mg; Sodium 320mg; Total Carbohydrate 20g (Dietary Fiber 1g, Sugars 9g); Protein 18g

Almond Float *(photo: page 66)*

Serve this delightful dessert with fortune cookies.

Ingredients:

- 1 (8-ounce) can pineapple chunks
- 2 (11-ounce) cans lichee nuts
- 1 (11-ounce) can mandarin oranges
- $\frac{1}{2}$ small jar maraschino cherries
- 1 envelope unflavored gelatin
- 1 cup water
- $\frac{1}{4}$ cup sugar
- $\frac{1}{2}$ cup lowfat milk or soy milk
- 1 teaspoon almond extract

Preparation:

- Oil a 1-quart gelatin mold or dish lightly and set aside.
- Place the pineapple, lichee nuts, mandarin oranges and maraschino cherries in the refrigerator to chill.

Procedure:

1. Sprinkle the gelatin over 1 cup water in a 1-quart saucepan.
2. Heat the gelatin mixture over medium heat, stirring until the gelatin dissolves completely. Add the sugar and stir until the sugar dissolves. Remove from the heat. Stir in the milk and the almond extract.
3. Pour the gelatin mixture into the prepared gelatin mold and chill for 4 hours or until firm.
4. Unmold the gelatin and cut into small cubes or diamonds.
5. Place the gelatin cubes in a large bowl placed over crushed ice. Add the chilled fruit and nuts, mix gently and spoon into dessert bowls. Serve immediately.

YIELD: *6 servings.* **Nutritional Facts Per Serving:** Calories 200; Total Fat 1g (Saturated Fat 0g); Cholesterol 0mg; Sodium 55mg; Total Carbohydrate 49g (Dietary Fiber 3g, Sugars 26g); Protein 3g

Almond Float is served at every formal banquet. It is usually served after the fifth course to refresh the palate and increase appetite. Four courses follow to complete the banquet.

Wonton Soup (photo: page 66)

Ingredients:

4 ounces fresh or frozen unpeeled shrimp

8 ounces lean ground pork

1 egg

1 tablespoon soy sauce

1½ teaspoons rice wine or pale dry sherry

¼ teaspoon sugar

2 slices fresh gingerroot, minced

1 teaspoon cornstarch

1 teaspoon water

Salt and pepper to taste

½ package wonton skins

4 cups chicken broth or Clear Steamed Soup Stock (page 28)

White of 1 green onion, diced into ¼-inch cubes

4 tablespoons finely shredded spinach or Chinese cabbage leaves

2 teaspoons sesame oil

Preparation:

- Peel and clean the shrimp and chop finely.
- Combine the shrimp, pork, egg, soy sauce, rice wine, sugar, gingerroot, cornstarch, water and salt and pepper in a bowl and mix well. Reserve half the mixture for the Fried Wontons (page 33).

- Prepare the wontons by keeping the wonton skins and filled wontons covered with a moist cloth to prevent drying. Prepare one wonton at a time. Place about 1 teaspoon of the pork and shrimp mixture in the center of each wonton skin. Moisten the edges of the skin with cold water, fold the wonton skin over to enclose the filling, press the edges together to seal, and shape by drawing the ends toward each other to curve the top edge slightly.

(See illustration on opposite page.)

Procedure:

1. Bring several quarts of water to a boil in a large kettle. Add the filled wontons to the boiling water carefully. When the water returns to the boil, add ½ cup cold water. The wontons are cooked when they rise to the top. Remove from the water with a strainer.

2. Strain the broth or stock into a saucepan and heat to serving temperature. Ladle the hot broth into serving bowls and add the wontons.

3. Sprinkle the green onion and spinach on the top and sprinkle with a few drops of sesame oil. Add a few strips of barbecue roast pork for garnish, if available. Serve immediately.

A package of frozen wonton skins contains approximately 45 skins. Remove the wonton skins from the freezer to thaw overnight in the refrigerator or for about 2 hours at room temperature. Use half the package for preparing the wontons for the wonton soup and the remaining wonton skins for the Fried Wontons (page 33). Also cut a few wonton skins into strips and deep-fry for making Crispy Noodles.

YIELD: *6 servings.* **Nutritional Facts Per Serving:** Calories 160; Total Fat 7g (Saturated Fat 2.5g); Cholesterol 65mg; Sodium 740mg; Total Carbohydrate 10g (Dietary Fiber 0g, Sugars 0g); Protein 13g

Fried Wontons *(photo: page 66)*

Use the half package of wonton skins remaining from the Wonton Soup (page 32) and the reserved wonton filling.

Preparation:
- Shape the wontons by placing a teaspoon of the filling in the center of each wonton skin, moisten the edges of the square with water and fold over to form a triangle and enclose the filling, sealing tightly. Make a pleat in each side of the triangle, drawing the points together and then opening slightly to resemble a tulip.

Procedure:
- Slip about a third of the wontons carefully into 350-degree deep peanut or soybean oil and deep-fry for 3 minutes or until crisp and golden brown. (The remaining two batches should each require only about 2 minutes deep-frying.) Remove with a strainer to paper towels to drain and serve immediately with golden plum sauce (duck sauce) and Chinese Hot Mustard Sauce.

YIELD: *6 servings.* **Nutritional Facts Per Serving:** Calories 220; Total Fat 13g (Saturated Fat 4g); Cholesterol 95mg; Sodium 210mg; Total Carbohydrate 12g (Dietary Fiber 1g, Sugars 0g) Protein 13g

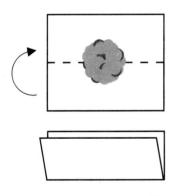
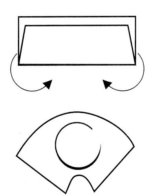

Chinese Hot Mustard Sauce

Ingredients:
1 tablespoon dry mustard powder
4 1/2 teaspoons cold water

Procedure:
- Combine the dry mustard and water and mix until smooth and creamy.

Serve Fried Wontons as an appetizer or Dim-sum.

Egg Rolls (Spring Rolls) *(photo: page 66)*

Egg rolls are deep-fried meat and vegetable-filled pastries. They make a very elegant and delightful dish traditionally served at parties and banquets.

The original name, Spring Rolls, comes from the tradition of serving them as appetizers on Chinese New Year which marks the beginning of spring.

Ingredients:

6 to 8 dried black mushrooms
$1/2$ cup boiling water
2 teaspoons cornstarch
8 ounces lean ground pork
1 teaspoon cornstarch
1 teaspoon soy sauce
1 cup chopped peeled shrimp
1 teaspoon rice wine or pale dry sherry
1 teaspoon cornstarch
$1/2$ cup bamboo shoots
$1/4$ cup water chestnuts
1 cup cabbage
$1/2$ cup celery
$1/2$ cup onion
$1/4$ cup carrot
2 tablespoons flour
2 tablespoons water
2 tablespoons peanut, corn or
    vegetable oil
2 slices fresh gingerroot, minced
$1/2$ teaspoon sugar
Salt to taste
8 ounces fresh bean sprouts
20 square egg roll skins
6 cups (about) oil for deep-frying

Preparation:

- Place the black mushrooms in a small bowl. Add the boiling water and let stand for 20 minutes. Drain and squeeze the mushrooms and reserve the liquid. Divide the reserved liquid into two portions. Blend 2 teaspoons cornstarch into one of the portions and set both portions aside.
- Trim off the mushroom stems and discard. Shred the mushroom caps finely and set aside.
- Mix the pork with 1 teaspoon cornstarch and 1 teaspoon soy sauce and set aside.

- Combine the shrimp, rice wine and 1 teaspoon cornstarch and set aside.
- Cut the bamboo shoots, water chestnuts, cabbage, celery, onion and carrot into small shreds resembling matchsticks and set aside.
- Blend 2 tablespoons flour with 2 tablespoons water to prepare a sealing paste for the egg rolls and set aside.

Procedure:

1. Heat the 2 tablespoons oil in a wok. Add the gingerroot and stir-fry until fragrant. Add the pork mixture and stir-fry until the pork turns white. Add the bamboo shoots, shredded mushrooms, the shrimp mixture, the reserved plain mushroom liquid, $1/2$ teaspoon sugar and salt to taste and stir-fry until well mixed.

2. Add the remaining shredded vegetables and stir-fry for several seconds. Add the cornstarch and mushroom liquid mixture and mix well.

3. Add the bean sprouts, cook for only a few seconds and remove from the heat to cool.

4. Place an egg roll skin on the work surface with the points of the square pointing in four directions. Moisten the edges with the sealing paste. Place 2 tablespoons of the filling in the center. Fold the bottom corner over the filling and tuck the corner around the filling. Fold the side corners over the filling and roll up, pressing the edges to seal. (See illustration on opposite page.)

♪. Heat the 6 cups oil for deep-frying to 375 degrees in a wok or deep fryer. Add the egg rolls carefully; do not crowd. Deep-fry for about 2 minutes or until golden brown. Drain well on paper towels.

6. Serve immediately with duck sauce or plum sauce and oriental hot mustard for dipping.

YIELD: 6 servings. **Nutritional Facts Per Serving:** 320 Calories; Total Fat 22g (Saturated Fat 5g); Cholesterol 90mg; Sodium 160mg; Total Carbohydrate 12g (Dietary Fiber 3g, Sugars 4g); Protein 19g

Fried Rice (Subgum) *(photo: page 66)*

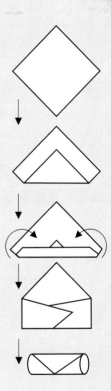

Ingredients:

- ¹/₂ cup shrimp, crab meat or lobster
- ¹/₂ cup diced meat (chicken, pork, turkey, beef, ham or sausage)
- 2 tablespoons mushrooms
- ¹/₄ cup bamboo shoots
- ¹/₄ cup each chopped whites and greens of scallions
- 4 cups cooked rice (see #1 at right)
- 4 tablespoons peanut, corn or vegetable oil
- 2 tablespoons frozen green peas
- ¹/₂ cup fresh bean sprouts
- 2 eggs, beaten
- 2 tablespoons soy sauce

Preparation:

- Rinse the fresh shrimp with 1 teaspoon baking soda dissolved in 1 cup water, rinse with clear cold water and pat dry. Cut into ¹/₃-inch chunks and set aside.
- Cut the meat, mushrooms, bamboo shoots and whites and greens of scallions into ¹/₃-inch chunks and set aside. Keep each ingredient separate.
- Pat all the vegetables dry and set aside.

Procedure:

1. The cooked rice cannot be too soft, so prepare according to the recipe for Steamed White Rice (page 26) with the following modifications: Cook the rice for 5 minutes. Wrap the pan lid with a cloth to absorb the moisture, replace the lid and set aside until cool or, remove from the heat and let stand uncovered until cool. (Or use the leftover rice from last night.)

2. Heat the wok over high heat. Add 2 tablespoons of the oil and the whites of scallions. Stir-fry for several seconds. Add the meat, shrimp, mushrooms, bamboo shoots and salt to taste and stir-fry until the meat is cooked. Add the peas and bean sprouts and remove to a plate.

3. Heat the wok and add the remaining 2 tablespoons oil. Scramble the eggs. Add the rice, soy sauce, scallions and mix well. Add the meat mixture and stir-fry for 30 seconds. Add the greens of the scallions and serve immediately.

YIELD: *4 servings.* **Nutritional Facts Per Serving:** Calories 410; Total Fat 5g (Saturated Fat 1.5g); Cholesterol 30mg; Sodium 1780mg; Total Carbohydrate 66g (Dietary Fiber 2g, Sugars 0g); Protein 22g
The sodium value is for regular soy sauce; using lite soy sauce would reduce the sodium content to 540mg.

Advanced

Classic Mandarin Cuisine

Butterfly Shrimp

Ingredients:

20 large shrimp
Salt to taste
1 teaspoon baking soda
1/4 cup water

Sauce:

1 tablespoon vegetable oil
2 tablespoons ketchup
1 teaspoon Hoisin sauce
1 cup water
1 tablespoon light soy sauce
2 1/2 tablespoons rice vinegar
1/4 cup sugar
Salt to taste

1 tablespoon cornstarch
2 tablespoons water

Batter:

1 cup flour
1 tablespoon baking powder
1/4 teaspoon salt
1 cup water

4 cups peanut, vegetable or corn
    oil for deep-frying

Preparation:

- Peel the shrimp, leaving the tails on.
  Make a cut lengthwise down the
  center of the back of each shrimp to,
  but not through, the other side to
  butterfly. Remove the dark veins, rinse
  well and pat dry. Sprinkle with salt to
  taste, baking soda and 1/4 cup water.
  Let stand for 30 minutes. (The soda
  will make the shrimp crisp.)

- Prepare the Sauce mixture by
  combining the 1 tablespoon vegetable
  oil, ketchup and Hoisin sauce in a
  saucepan and heat over medium heat
  until well blended, stirring constantly.
  Add 1 cup water, light soy sauce,
  rice vinegar, sugar and salt to taste
  and blend well. Bring the Sauce to a
  simmer. Blend the cornstarch with
  2 tablespoons water and stir into
  the simmering sauce. Cook until
  thickened, stirring constantly. Set
  the sauce aside to keep warm.

- Prepare the Batter by mixing the
  flour, baking powder and 1/4 teaspoon
  salt together in a medium bowl.
  Add 1 cup water gradually, stirring
  constantly until the Batter is smooth
  and well blended.

Procedure:

1. Rinse the shrimp under cold running
   water to remove all the baking soda,
   drain well and pat dry.

2. Heat the peanut oil in a wok or deep
   fryer almost to the smoking point.

3. Dip the shrimp one at a time into the
   prepared Batter and place in the hot
   oil. Do not crowd the shrimp in the hot
   oil. Deep-fry until golden brown and
   drain on paper towels.

4. Serve the shrimp immediately with the
   warm Sauce.

YIELD: *5 servings.* **Nutritional Facts Per Serving:** Calories 450; Total Fat 15g (Saturated Fat 2.5g);
Cholesterol 160mg; Sodium 1010mg; Total Carbohydrate 53g (Dietary Fiber 1 g, Sugars 5g); Protein 26g

Chinese Cabbage in Chicken Sauce

Ingredients:

3 dried black mushrooms
$1/2$ cup chicken stock
$1/2$ teaspoon salt
$1/2$ teaspoon sugar
$1 1/2$ teaspoons cornstarch
1 tablespoon water
$1 1/2$ pounds Chinese cabbage
   (Napa or celery cabbage)
4 tablespoons vegetable oil
2 slices fresh gingerroot, minced
6 ($1/2 \times 1$-inch) pieces cooked ham
1 tablespoon vegetable oil
$1 1/2$ teaspoons rice wine or pale
   dry sherry

Preparation:

- Soak the mushrooms in boiling water to cover for 15 minutes. Drain and squeeze dry, trim the stems, slice the mushroom caps into fourths and set aside.

- Combine the chicken stock, salt and sugar in a small bowl and stir until the salt and sugar dissolve. Set this mixture aside.

- Blend the cornstarch with the water and set aside.

- Cut the Chinese cabbage lengthwise into halves. Stack the halves together and then cut diagonally crosswise into $1/2 \times 2$-inch pieces. Stir-fry in 4 tablespoons of the vegetable oil for several seconds. Add the chicken stock mixture and cook for 2 minutes. Remove the cabbage mixture from the heat and remove the cabbage to a platter using a slotted spoon. Pour the chicken stock into a bowl and set aside.

Procedure:

1. Stir-fry the gingerroot, mushroom slices and ham in 1 tablespoon vegetable oil for several seconds.

2. Add the rice wine, cabbage and the reserved chicken stock and bring to a boil.

3. Stir in the cornstarch mixture and cook until the sauce is slightly thickened, stirring constantly. Serve immediately.

YIELD: *6 servings.* **Nutritional Facts Per Serving:** Calories 100; Total Fat 9g (Saturated Fat 1g); Cholesterol 0mg; Sodium 280mg; Total Carbohydrate 4g (Dietary Fiber 1g, Sugars 1g); Protein 2g

Egg Foo Yung (Canton School) *(photo: page 67)*

Ingredients:

1 cup fresh bean sprouts
1 tablespoon chopped green onions
1 tablespoon shredded bamboo shoots
1 tablespoon finely chopped water
    chestnuts
1/4 cup shredded celery (no leaves)
2 tablespoons sliced fresh mushrooms
1/2 cup shredded cooked meat (pork,
    beef, chicken, crab meat, shrimp)
6 eggs
1 teaspoon salt
1/4 teaspoon sugar
Dash of pepper
1/2 teaspoon baking soda
1/2 cup vegetable oil
Sauce for Egg Foo Yung (below)

Preparation:

- Rinse the fresh bean sprouts in cold water in a bowl, discard husks that float to the surface, drain and pat dry.
- Shred the vegetables and meat uniformly and combine in a bowl.

- Beat the eggs in a small bowl. Add the salt, sugar, pepper and baking soda and mix well.
- Add the egg mixture to the vegetable mixture and stir gently until well mixed.

Procedure:

1. Preheat a wok over high heat for 30 seconds. Pour 2 tablespoons of the oil into the wok, swirl the oil in the pan and heat for 30 seconds but do not allow the oil to smoke.
2. Pour 1/2 cup of the egg mixture carefully into the wok. Cook until the mixture is brown on one side, turn over and brown on the other side. Remove from the wok and place in a dish.
3. Repeat the cooking procedure with the remaining oil and egg mixture.
4. Stack the foo yungs in a serving dish and pour the Sauce over the top. Serve immediately.

Sauce for Egg Foo Yung

Ingredients:

1 tablespoon cornstarch
1 tablespoon cold water
1 cup chicken stock
1 tablespoon low-sodium soy sauce or
    1 1/2 teaspoons regular soy sauce
1/2 teaspoon sugar

Preparation:

- Blend the cornstarch and water together in a small bowl and set aside.

Procedure:

1. Bring the chicken stock to a boil in a small saucepan.
2. Add the soy sauce, sugar and the cornstarch blended with water. Reduce the heat and cook until thickened, stirring constantly. Remove from the heat and set aside to keep warm.

Egg Foo Yung means egg blossom.

Make a nutritional omelet dish with leftover cooked meat cut into small chunks and fresh vegetables cut into small shreds.

The picture of the omelet resembles a blossom—a hibiscus.

YIELD: *4 servings.* **Nutritional Facts Per Serving:** Calories 370; Total Fat 32g (Saturated Fat 4g); Cholesterol 290mg; Sodium 1340mg; Total Carbohydrate 5g (Dietary Fiber 1g, Sugars 1g); Protein 16g

Clear Steamed Fish *(photo: page 67)*

Ingredients:

2 tablespoons light soy sauce

1/4 teaspoon sugar

1 teaspoon sesame oil

1 (1-pound) fish

1 teaspoon salt

1 tablespoon rice wine or pale dry sherry

1 teaspoon vegetable oil

1 teaspoon cornstarch

1 garlic clove

2 slices fresh gingerroot

1 green onion

1 tablespoon fermented black beans

Preparation:

- Combine the soy sauce, sugar and sesame oil in a small bowl and blend well to make the dipping sauce. Set the sauce aside.
- Clean the fish inside and out and pat dry with a paper towel. Make several diagonal slashes over the body of the fish. Rub the fish inside and out with the salt.
- Mix the rice wine, vegetable oil and cornstarch together and rub the inside and outside of the fish with the mixture.
- Crush the garlic and shred the gingerroot and green onion. Place the garlic inside the fish and insert the gingerroot and green onion in the diagonal slashes. Sprinkle the fish with the fermented black beans.

Procedure:

1. Place the fish in foil, then in a steamer and steam for 20 minutes or until the fish flakes easily.
2. Serve the fish immediately with the dipping sauce.

YIELD: *4 servings.* **Nutritional Facts Per Serving:** Calories 130; Total Fat 4g (Saturated Fat 1.5g); Cholesterol 90mg; Sodium 810mg; Total Carbohydrate 2g (Dietary Fiber 0g, Sugars 0g); Protein 20g

Use the whole fish for both presentation and the special sweet flavor that makes this dish truly gourmet and festive. Traditional for Chinese New Year, it signifies the Beginning (the head) and the End (the tail).

Cantonese Barbecue Roast Pork *(photo: page 67)*

Try serving this delicious roast as an appetizer by slicing thinly and serving with a dipping sauce made of plum sauce and soy sauce blended with a few drops of sesame oil or Chinese mustard.

Ingredients:

1 (1¼-pound) lean boneless pork loin
2 tablespoons rice wine or pale
   dry sherry
¼ cup soy sauce
2 tablespoons Hoisin sauce
2 tablespoons honey
1 teaspoon sugar
2 green onions
3 slices fresh gingerroot
2 garlic cloves, crushed
1 tablespoon sesame oil
1½ teaspoons honey
1½ teaspoons hot water

Preparation:

- Cut or tie the pork into a piece that is 1 inch thick, 2 inches wide and 6 inches long. Place the pork in a dish.
- Combine the rice wine, soy sauce, Hoisin sauce, 2 tablespoons honey and sugar in a small bowl. Shred the green onions, gingerroot and garlic and add to the mixture.
- Pour the marinade over the pork, turning to coat well. Marinate in the refrigerator for 3 to 6 hours but no longer.
- Blend the sesame oil, 1½ teaspoons honey and hot water in a small bowl to make a glaze and set aside.

Procedure:

1. Drain the pork and reserve the marinade for basting. Place the pork strips onto the upper oven rack over a pan placed on the lower rack to catch the dripping juices. Add water to the pan to provide steam to moisten the pork during cooking.
2. Turn the oven to 400 degrees. Roast for 30 minutes.
3. Reduce the oven temperature to 350 degrees. Roast for 30 minutes longer, basting occasionally with the reserved marinade.
4. Remove the pork from the oven and brush on all sides with the prepared sesame oil glaze. Let the pork stand for several minutes for easier, neater slicing.

The pork may also be prepared in a microwave oven. Use only microwave-safe cooking utensils. Microwave on High for 10 minutes, baste, turn the pork over and microwave for 15 minutes longer or to 165 degrees on a meat thermometer.

YIELD: *6 servings.* **Nutritional Facts Per Serving:** Calories 180; Total Fat 7g (Saturated Fat 2g); Cholesterol 60mg; Sodium 410mg; Total Carbohydrate 7g (Dietary Fiber 0g, Sugars 7g); Protein 21g

Roast Pork Lo-Mein (Taiwanese-Style) *(photo: page 67)*

Ingredients:

4 dried black mushrooms
5 to 6 ounces Chinese cabbage
  (celery cabbage or bok choy)
1/2 cup canned bamboo shoots
8 ounces roast pork
2 green onions
9 ounces Chinese egg noodles
1 tablespoon peanut oil
1 tablespoon sesame oil
2 tablespoons peanut, corn or
  vegetable oil
2 slices fresh gingerroot, minced
1 teaspoon salt
2 tablespoons soy sauce
1/2 cup bean sprouts
1 teaspoon sugar
Dash of black pepper

Preparation:

- Soak the mushrooms in 1 cup boiling water for 15 minutes. Drain the mushrooms, trim off the stems, cut the caps into 1/8-inch strips and set aside.
- Slice the cabbage into 1/4 × 1/4 × 2-inch pieces and set aside.
- Shred the bamboo shoots into 1/8 × 2-inch shreds and set aside.
- Cut the roast pork into 1/4 × 1/4 × 2-inch strips to yield about 1 1/2 cups.
- Dice the white of the green onions into 1/4-inch pieces and cut the green tops into 1-inch shreds. Set the white and green portions aside separately.
- Arrange the remaining ingredients in order for quick addition to the wok.

Procedure:

1. Bring 2 quarts of water or more to a boil in a large deep saucepan. Add the Chinese noodles and stir gently while the noodles are cooking to loosen. Cook for 3 minutes, stirring gently. Drain the noodles and spread on a large platter. Drizzle with 1 tablespoon peanut oil and 1 tablespoon sesame oil to prevent sticking.

2. Heat a wok over high heat. Add 2 tablespoons peanut oil, gingerroot and the white portion of the green onions and stir-fry for several seconds.

3. Add the mushrooms. cabbage and bamboo shoots and stir-fry for 2 minutes.

4. Add the salt and soy sauce and stir-fry for several seconds.

5. Add the bean sprouts, roast pork and the cooked noodles. Sprinkle with the sugar and pepper. Stir-fry gently for several seconds by lifting and mixing with cooking chopsticks and a turner.

6. Garnish with green onion shreds and stir-fry for 1 minute. Serve immediately.

7. Note: For a recipe for Chinese Fresh Noodles, see page 98.

YIELD: *5 servings.* **Nutritional Facts Per Serving:** Calories 220; Total Fat 13g (Saturated Fat 1.5g); Cholesterol 25mg; Sodium 970mg; Total Carbohydrate 19g (Dietary Fiber 2g, Sugars 2g); Protein 8g

Genghis Khan Barbecue (photo: page 68)

Ingredients:

8 ounces lean beef, lamb, chicken or shrimp
$1/4$ cup soy sauce
$1/3$ cup rice wine
1 tablespoon sesame oil
1 teaspoon hot bean sauce
$1/2$ teaspoon sugar
2 whole red chili peppers
1 garlic clove, crushed
1 green bell pepper
1 tomato
2 tablespoons thinly sliced water chestnuts
6 fresh mushrooms or Chinese straw mushrooms
5 to 6 ounces Chinese cabbage
2 green onions

Preparation:

- Cut the beef into $1/4 \times 1 \times 2$-inch strips and place in a bowl.
- Combine the soy sauce, rice wine, sesame oil, hot bean sauce, sugar, chili peppers and garlic in a small bowl and mix well. Pour the marinade over the meat and mix well. Marinate for 10 minutes.
- Discard the seeds and membranes from the green pepper and core the tomato. Cut the green pepper, tomato, water chestnuts, mushrooms, cabbage and green onions into 2-inch shreds and set aside.

Procedure:

1. Preheat the barbecue pan over medium-high heat. Drain the beef, reserving the marinade. Arrange the beef strips on the dome of the pan and cook until lightly braised, turning constantly, bring the strips to the bottom of the reservoir pan and then remove to the center of a serving dish.

2. Layer the cabbage, green pepper and water chestnuts on the barbecue pan and top with the mushrooms, green onions and tomato. Cook for 3 to 5 minutes, basting with the reserved marinade. Place the vegetables around the beef.

3. Serve the beef and vegetables immediately with steamed rice.

YIELD: *6 servings.* **Nutritional Facts Per Serving:** Calories 130; Total Fat 6g (Saturated Fat 2g); Cholesterol 25mg; Sodium 420mg; Total Carbohydrate 7g (Dietary Fiber 1g, Sugars 2g); Protein 12g

The original cast-iron barbecue pan was a replica of Genghis Khan's infantry helmet. The belief is that his hungry infantry would remove the helmets after a hard day of fighting and cook along the road. Later, the Chinese followed the lead of the Mongolians and converted the helmet into a unique, thermo-efficient, healthy cooking utensil. The result is a dome-shaped pan with a flaired lip around the outside that catches the fat and juices flowing via channels in the pan from the food being grilled on the dome. The heat is supplied by fire under the dome, which is perforated with holes for heat and smoke to rise under and around the thin strips of meat placed on the dome. A modern version of this ancient utensil can be used on any type of stove or hibachi.

Chiao-Tzu Northern Dumplings (photo: page 68)

The dumplings can also be cooked in a steamer for 25 minutes. The cooked dumplings can then be fried with 2 tablespoons vegetable oil and a little water to make Pan-Fried Dumplings, also called Pot Stickers.

Chiao-Tzu is a staple food to Northern Chinese. This is made of wheat flour and water only.

The stuffings are ground pork and Chinese cabbage with a touch of ginger and garlic.

The dumplings are a nutritional one-dish meal.

Ingredients:

Dough:
2 cups sifted all-purpose flour
³/4 cup boiling water

8 ounces Chinese cabbage
1 pound lean ground pork
1 teaspoon freshly minced gingerroot
1 garlic clove, minced
1 tablespoon rice wine or pale
    dry sherry
1 tablespoon soy sauce
1 teaspoon salt
1 tablespoon sesame oil

Dipping Sauce:
¹/4 cup soy sauce
2 tablespoons rice vinegar

Preparation

- Place the flour in a bowl. Add the boiling water gradually and mix and knead until a smooth dough forms. Cover the Dough with a moist cloth and let stand for 30 minutes.
- Turn the Dough onto a lightly floured surface and knead for 3 minutes.
- Let the Dough rest for 30 minutes to become softer and more pliable.
- Rinse the cabbage under cold running water and pat dry with paper towels. Discard the wilted leaves and root end. Slice and chop the cabbage very finely and set aside.
- Combine the ground pork, gingerroot, garlic, wine, 1 tablespoon soy sauce, salt and sesame oil in a bowl and mix well. Add the chopped cabbage and mix well.
- Blend ¹/4 cup soy sauce and rice vinegar in a small bowl. Set aside to be used as a Dipping Sauce for the finished dumplings.

Procedure:

1. Divide the dough into two portions and shape each into a log about 1 inch in diameter. Cut each log into 12 equal portions using the cleaver.

2. Flatten each portion in the palm of your hand to a circle ¼ inch thick and then roll on a lightly floured surface into a 3-inch circle only ⅛ inch thick.

3. Place 1 tablespoon of the pork mixture in the center of each circle and bring the dough up to enclose the filling, pinching the top edges together and pleating the edges to shape into a small pouch.

4. Place the shaped dumpling on a platter and cover with a moist cloth to prevent drying while shaping the remaining dumplings.

5. Bring 2 quarts of water or more to a bubbling boil in a deep saucepan. Add the dumplings one at a time to the boiling water and turn over gently with a strainer to prevent the dumplings from sticking together.

6. Cover the saucepan and cook over high heat just until the water returns to the boil. Add 1 cup cold water, cover the saucepan and return to the boil.

7. Remove the dumplings from the water with a bamboo strainer, arrange on a platter and serve immediately with the prepared Dipping Sauce.

YIELD: *5 servings.* **Nutritional Facts Per Serving:** Calories 450; Total Fat 23g (Saturated Fat 8g); Cholesterol 65mg; Sodium 750mg; Total Carbohydrate 40g (Dietary Fiber 2g, Sugars 1g); Protein 21g

Mandarin Thin Pancakes (Pao-Ping) *(photo: page 68)*

These pancakes are traditionally eaten with Moo Shi Pork (page 47) and Peking Duck (page 106). Thin pancakes can be made ahead, frozen and steamed for 10 minutes before serving. Making them requires practice in order to make the dough paper-thin. Use enough sesame oil between the pancakes to allow the two pancakes to separate when heated.

Ingredients:

1³/₄ cups all-purpose flour
³/₄ cup boiling water
Scallions for garnish
2 tablespoons sesame oil

Spreading Sauce:
3 tablespoons Hoisin sauce
1 teaspoon sugar
1 teaspoon soy sauce
1 teaspoon sesame oil

Preparation:

* Place the flour in a bowl. Add the boiling water gradually, mixing with a wooden spoon or cooking chopstick. Knead on a surface lightly sprinkled with cornstarch for 5 minutes or until smooth. Cover the dough with a moist cloth and let stand for 30 minutes.
* Prepare scallion brushes by cutting enough scallions into 3-inch pieces to yield 12 pieces. Cut many parallel cuts for 1 inch on either end of each piece and place in ice water. Let the scallions stand in the ice water until serving time; the thin cuts will separate and open to resemble flowers.
* Prepare the Spreading Sauce by blending the Hoisin sauce, sugar, soy sauce and 1 teaspoon sesame oil in a small dish and set aside.

Procedure:

1. Knead the prepared dough on a lightly floured surface for 3 minutes. Shape into a rope about 1-inch in diameter and 12 inches long.
2. Cut into 12 portions if the pancakes are to be served with Moo Shi Pork or into 24 portions if they are to be served with Peking Duck.
3. Shape and flatten each portion of the dough into a round cake between the palms of the hands. Brush one side of each cake evenly with some of the 2 tablespoons sesame oil. Place two of the cakes with the oiled sides together and roll each pair evenly into a flat thin 8-inch pancake.
4. Preheat an ungreased griddle over medium-low heat. Place each paired pancake on the hot griddle. Bake for about 1 minute or until light brown spots appear on the bottom, turn over and bake for about 30 seconds longer.
5. Pull the pancakes apart into two thin cakes and pile on a plate. Steam for about 10 minutes, garnish with the scallions and serve immediately with the Spreading Sauce.

YIELD: *6 servings.* **Nutritional Facts Per Serving:** Calories 170; Total Fat 5g (Saturated Fat 0.5g); Cholesterol 0mg; Sodium 0mg; Total Carbohydrate 28g (Dietary Fiber 0g, Sugars 0g); Protein 4g

Moo Shi Pork *(photo: page 68)*

Ingredients:

- ¹/₄ cup dried wood ears (black fungus)
- ¹/₂ cup dried golden needles
  (tiger lily buds)
- 4 ounces lean pork
- 1 tablespoon rice wine or pale
  dry sherry
- 1 tablespoon soy sauce
- ¹/₄ teaspoon sugar
- 1 teaspoon cornstarch
- White of 1 scallion
- 3 tablespoons vegetable oil
- 2 eggs, beaten
- 1 slice fresh gingerroot, minced
- 1 teaspoon salt
- 1 recipe Mandarin Thin Pancakes
  (page 46)

Preparation:

- Place the wood ears and golden
  needles in a small bowl. Add enough
  boiling water to cover and let stand
  for 15 minutes. Drain, rinse, pat dry
  and set aside.
- Cut the pork into shreds to yield
  ¹/₂ cup. Place in a bowl and add the
  rice wine, soy sauce, sugar and
  cornstarch and mix well.
- Cut the scallion into shreds and
  set aside.

Procedure:

1. Heat 2 tablespoons of the oil in a
   wok over medium heat. Add the eggs
   and scramble or cook in a thin sheet
   and cut into strips. Remove the eggs
   to a platter.
2. Add the remaining 1 tablespoon oil to
   the wok. Add the gingerroot, scallion
   and pork mixture and stir-fry for
   several minutes.
3. Add the wood ears, golden needles and
   salt and stir-fry for 3 minutes.
4. Return the eggs to the wok and mix
   gently but thoroughly.
5. Serve with the Mandarin Thin
   Pancakes.

*Wood ears and golden
needles can be
purchased at Asian
food markets and are
described in more
detail in the Szechuan
and Hunan Levels.*

YIELD: *6 servings.* **Nutritional Facts Per Serving:** Calories 140; Total Fat 11g (Saturated Fat 2g);
Cholesterol 155mg; Sodium 620mg; Total Carbohydrate 1g (Dietary Fiber 0g, Sugars 0g); Protein 9g

Gourmet I

Features famous gourmet dishes from all five regional schools, the last two lessons are Dim-Sum

Lemon Chicken (Eastern Cuisine) *(photo: page 69)*

Gourmet dishes are noted for excellent taste and more elaborate presentations. Some recipes are not difficult but require beautiful garnishes.

Ingredients:

2 whole chicken breasts
Salt and pepper to taste
1 tablespoon rice wine or pale
   dry sherry
Juice of 1/2 lemon
1 large tomato
2 tablespoons ketchup
1 tablespoon soy sauce
1 tablespoon sesame oil
4 1/2 teaspoons vinegar
1 1/2 teaspoons sugar
1/4 cup flour
1/4 cup cornstarch
1 egg
4 cups vegetable oil for frying
4 cups shredded lettuce
Lemon juice to taste
1/2 lemon, thinly sliced
Parsley
2 tablespoons vegetable oil

Preparation:

- Split the chicken breasts, skin and bone and place in a shallow dish. Sprinkle with salt and pepper, rice wine and lemon juice. Marinate the chicken in the refrigerator for 20 minutes.
- Core the tomato and cut into a number of thin wedges to but not through the bottom to resemble a flower and set aside.
- Combine the ketchup, soy sauce, sesame oil, vinegar and sugar in a small dish, blend well and set aside.
- Mix the flour and cornstarch together on parchment paper or foil. Beat the egg in a shallow dish.
- Dip each chicken breast into the beaten egg and roll in the flour and cornstarch mixture to coat well.

Procedure:

1. Heat the oil for frying in a large wok or pan over medium heat to 350 degrees. Add the prepared chicken to the hot oil and fry until lightly browned on all sides. Drain on paper towels and cut into bite-size pieces.

2. Arrange the chicken pieces on two opposite quadrants on the serving plate, leaving a small center area open. Fill the remaining quadrants with the shredded lettuce. Sprinkle the lettuce with lemon juice and arrange slightly overlapping lemon slices on top. Place the tomato flower in the center of the plate on a bed of parsley.

3. Heat the 2 tablespoons oil in a small saucepan. Add the ketchup mixture and heat, stirring constantly. Pour the hot mixture over the chicken and serve immediately.

YIELD: *6 servings.* **Nutritional Facts Per Serving:** Calories 300; Total Fat 17g (Saturated Fat 2.5g); Cholesterol 55mg; Sodium 180mg; Total Carbohydrate 12g (Dietary Fiber 0g; Sugars 2g); Protein 24g

Beef in Oyster Sauce (Cantonese Cuisine)

Ingredients:

12 ounces lean flank or top round steak

Marinade:
$1/2$ teaspoon salt
$1/2$ teaspoon baking soda
$1/2$ teaspoon baking powder
$1^1/2$ teaspoons soy sauce
1 tablespoon rice wine or pale dry sherry
1 tablespoon cornstarch
3 tablespoons water

$1^1/2$ teaspoons vegetable oil

Oyster Sauce:
$1/2$ teaspoon sugar
1 teaspoon sesame oil
1 teaspoon cornstarch
$1^1/2$ teaspoons soy sauce
1 tablespoon oyster sauce
1 tablespoon water

6 cups vegetable oil for deep-frying
2 tablespoons vegetable oil
Whites of 2 green onions, diced
2 slices gingerroot, minced
$1^1/2$ teaspoons rice wine or pale dry sherry

Preparation:

- Cut the steak into $1/4 \times 1/2 \times 1^1/4$-inch pieces and place in a mixing bowl.
- Prepare the Marinade by combining the salt, baking soda, baking powder, $1^1/2$ teaspoons soy sauce, 1 tablespoon rice wine, 1 tablespoon cornstarch and 3 tablespoons water in a small dish and mix well. Add the Marinade to the steak and toss to coat. Drizzle with $1^1/2$ teaspoons oil and let stand for 30 minutes.
- Prepare the Oyster Sauce by combining the sugar, sesame oil, 1 teaspoon cornstarch, $1^1/2$ teaspoons soy sauce, oyster sauce and 1 tablespoon water in a small dish, mix well and set aside.

Procedure:

1. Heat the oil for deep-frying in a wok or deep fryer to 350 degrees. Add the steak pieces and deep fry until the steak changes color. Remove the beef from the hot oil and drain on paper towels in a colander.
2. Heat the wok until very hot. Add the 2 tablespoons oil, green onions and gingerroot . Stir-fry until fragrant.
3. Add the beef to the wok. Add the remaining $1^1/2$ teaspoons rice wine and the Oyster Sauce mixture. Stir-fry for several seconds and serve immediately.

YIELD: *6 servings.* **Nutritional Facts Per Serving:** Calories 220; Total Fat 18g (Saturated Fat 2.5g); Cholesterol 30mg; Sodium 620mg; Total Carbohydrate 3g (Dietary Fiber 0g; Sugars 0g); Protein 13g

Pearl Balls (Northern Cuisine) (Chen Chu Jou Wan) *(photo: page 69)*

Ingredients:

- ³/4 cups glutinous rice (sweet rice)
- 4 dried black mushrooms
- 1 tablespoon finely chopped water chestnuts
- 1 tablespoon finely chopped scallions
- 1/2 teaspoon finely chopped gingerroot
- 1 teaspoon salt
- 1 tablespoon sesame oil
- 4 1/2 teaspoons soy sauce
- 1/2 teaspoon sugar
- Dash of black pepper
- 2 tablespoons cornstarch
- 1 1/2 pounds lean ground pork

Preparation:

- Place the rice in a bowl and cover with a generous amount of water. Let stand to soak for 1 hour.
- Place the black mushrooms in a bowl and cover with boiling water. Let stand to soak for 15 minutes. Drain and squeeze dry, cut off and discard the stems and chop the caps finely.
- Combine the finely chopped mushroom caps with the water chestnuts, scallions and gingerroot in a small dish and set aside.
- Combine the salt, sesame oil, soy sauce, sugar and pepper in a small dish, mix well and set aside.
- Sprinkle the cornstarch evenly in a tray. Drain the rice and layer evenly over the cornstarch.

Procedure:

1. Combine the ground pork and the soy sauce mixture in a bowl and mix well by hand.
2. Add the mushroom mixture and mix well.
3. Shape the pork mixture into 1-inch balls. Place several of the balls in the prepared tray and rock the tray back and forth until the balls are covered with the rice. Repeat until all the balls are coated.
4. Pat and shape the balls to restore the round shape and place on a foil sheet with edges turned up inside a steamer or line the steamer with moist, oiled cheesecloth and place the balls directly on the cloth.
5. Steam for 40 minutes or until the rice is cooked.
6. Remove the balls to a serving plate and garnish with small thin carrot slices and parsley leaves on top. Serve immediately. May add carrot slices to the balls before steaming if desired and add the parsley leaf garnish after cooking.

YIELD: 5 *servings.* **Nutritional Facts Per Serving:** Calories 370; Total Fat 11g (Saturated Fat 3g); Cholesterol 85mg; Sodium 850mg; Total Carbohydrate 34g (Dietary Fiber 1g; Sugars 0g); Protein 32g

This truly gourmet dish is a favorite of Chinese emperors. The sweet rice is not only delicious but beautiful, resembling pearls. It is usually served as a banquet dish, especially for the New Year. If you wish to prepare it in advance and freeze, resteam for 15 minutes before serving.

Four Kinds of Braised Vegetables (Northern Cuisine) *(photo: page 69)*

Ingredients:

2 pounds hearts of any green
    vegetable, such as Chinese cabbage
3 firm tomatoes
4 cups soup stock
1½ teaspoons salt
1 teaspoon sugar
1 tablespoon cornstarch
1 tablespoon water
2 cups canned baby corn ears
2 cups canned straw mushrooms

Preparation:

- Cut the green vegetable into ¼ × ¾ ×
  4-inch pieces. Place the vegetable in a
  large strainer or colander and dip into
  a large pot of boiling water for several
  seconds to blanch. Plunge into ice
  water to stop the cooking, drain well
  and set aside.
- Place the tomatoes in boiling water for
  several seconds to loosen the skins.
  Drain the tomatoes, peel, cut into
  quarters and set aside.
- Combine the soup stock, salt and
  sugar in a saucepan and mix well.
  Remove 2 cups of the mixture to a
  second saucepan and set aside.
- Blend the cornstarch and water in
  a small bowl and set aside.

Procedure:

1. Bring the soup stock in one of the
   saucepans to a boil. Dip the vegetables,
   one kind at a time, into the soup
   stock. Cook the Chinese cabbage and
   baby corn for 2 minutes, the straw
   mushrooms for 1 minute, and a few
   seconds for the tomatoes. Remove,
   drain and arrange the vegetables on
   a serving platter.
2. Bring the second saucepan of the soup
   stock to a boil. Stir in the cornstarch
   mixture and cook until thickened
   stirring constantly.
3. Pour the thickened stock over the
   vegetables and serve immediately.

YIELD: *6 servings.* **Nutritional Facts Per Serving:** Calories 120; Total Fat 1.5g (Saturated Fat 0g); Cholesterol 0mg; Sodium 860mg; Total Carbohydrate 22g (Dietary Fiber 3g; Sugars 2g); Protein 6g

Paper-Wrapped Chicken (Shanghai-Eastern Cuisine) *(photo: page 69)*

Use your fingers to open the package, but use chopsticks in eating. Decorate the platter with fresh vegetables cut into the shapes of flowers.

Ingredients:

- 1 pound boneless skinless chicken breasts
- 1 tablespoon light soy sauce
- 1 tablespoon rice wine or pale dry sherry
- 1 teaspoon sugar
- 1/2 teaspoon salt
- 1/4 teaspoon black pepper
- Dash of ground ginger or 2 slices fresh gingerroot, minced
- 3 dried black mushrooms
- 2 ounces cooked ham
- 16 (6 × 6-inch) squares parchment paper
- 1 tablespoon sesame oil
- 16 Chinese parsley leaves
- 6 cups peanut, corn or vegetable oil for deep-frying

Preparation:

- Cut the chicken into 16 thin 1 1/2 × 2-inch pieces. Place the chicken in a bowl and add the soy sauce, rice wine, sugar, salt, pepper and ginger and mix until coated. Marinate in the refrigerator for about 20 minutes.
- Soak the mushrooms in boiling water for about 15 minutes. Drain the mushrooms, squeeze dry and cut off and discard the stems. Cut the mushroom caps into small triangles and set aside.
- Cut the ham into small triangles about the size of the mushroom triangles and set aside.

Procedure:

1. Place a square of parchment paper on the work surface with the corners pointing in the four directions. Brush the center of the parchment with a small amount of the sesame oil.

2. Place the front of a parsley leaf down in the center of the parchment. Place a few pieces of ham to one side of the parsley leaf and mushroom pieces to the other. Place a chicken piece on the top.

3. Fold the bottom corner over the chicken, then fold the left and right hand corners over to enclose the filling. Fold the remaining corner over and tuck inside to form a neat package.

4. Repeat with the remaining parchment and ingredients to make 16 packages.

5. Heat the oil for deep-frying in a wok to 300 to 350 degrees. Add the packages to the hot oil; do not crowd. Deep-fry for 1 1/2 to 2 minutes on each side, remove to drain on paper towels.

6. Place the packages on the serving platter and serve immediately.

This old classic cooking method is especially healthy. The rich juices contained within the package are delicious poured over steamed rice.

YIELD: 4 *servings.* **Nutritional Facts Per Serving:** Calories 220; Total Fat 9g (Saturated Fat 1.5g); Cholesterol 75mg; Sodium 710mg; Total Carbohydrate 4g (Dietary Fiber 0g; Sugars 1g); Protein 30g

Hot and Sour Soup (Szechuan Cuisine) *(photo: page 70)*

Wood ears, tiger lily stems, and flower pepper can be found at Asian food markets and are described in the Szechuan and Hunan Levels.

Ingredients:

2 dried black mushrooms
6 dried wood ear mushrooms
4 dried tiger lily stems
1 fresh soft bean curd (tofu)
$1/4$ cup pork
$1/3$ cup bamboo shoots
2 tablespoons cornstarch
3 tablespoons water
1 egg
1 tablespoon peanut, corn or
   vegetable oil
White of 1 green onion, diced
$1 1/2$ teaspoons hot bean sauce
2 tablespoons soy sauce
4 cups chicken broth
Salt to taste
2 tablespoons rice vinegar
$1/2$ teaspoon sugar
$1/2$ teaspoon black or white pepper
$1/4$ teaspoon crushed flower pepper
2 teaspoons sesame chili oil

Preparation:

* Combine the black and wood ear mushrooms and the tiger lily stems in a small bowl and cover with boiling water. Let stand for 15 minutes, drain and squeeze dry. Cut off and discard the mushroom stems and the harder portions of the wood ears. Shred the black mushroom caps and wood ears. Cut the tiger lily stems into halves and set aside.

* Shred the bean curd, pork and bamboo shoots into $1/4 \times 1/4 \times 1$-inch pieces and set aside.
* Dissolve the cornstarch in water and set aside.
* Beat the egg and set aside.

Procedure:

1. Preheat a wok. Add 1 tablespoon oil, green onion, shredded pork and hot bean sauce and stir-fry for several seconds until the pork is cooked.
2. Add the soy sauce, black mushrooms, wood ears, tiger lily stems and bamboo shoots and stir-fry for several seconds.
3. Add the chicken broth, salt, vinegar, sugar and peppers and mix well. Bring the mixture to a boil.
4. Stir the cornstarch mixture into the boiling broth. Cook until slightly thickened, stirring constantly.
5. Add the bean curd, return to a boil and turn off the heat. Drop the beaten egg through the cooking chopsticks and stir gently several times.
6. Add the sesame chili oil just before serving. Ladle into soup cups, garnish with a sprinkle of freshly minced coriander and green scallion tops.

YIELD: *6 servings.* **Nutritional Facts Per Serving:** Calories 140; Total Fat 8g (Saturated Fat 1.5g); Cholesterol 5mg; Sodium 800mg; Total Carbohydrate 6g (Dietary Fiber 1g; Sugars 0g); Protein 11g

Marble Eggs (Tea Leaf Eggs) *(photo: page 70)*

This popular cold appetizer is wonderful to serve at a picnic.

Ingredients:

5 to 10 eggs
1½ to 2 cups water
3 teabags (black tea only), or
    3 tablespoons loose tea leaves
1 tablespoon salt
3 tablespoons soy sauce
½ teaspoon five-spice powder

Procedure:

1. Place the eggs in a saucepan and add enough water to cover generously.
2. Bring the water to just below the boiling point over low heat and cook for 20 to 30 minutes or until the eggs are hard-cooked.
3. Place the eggs in the pan under cool running water until the eggs are cool.
4. Drain the eggs. Crack the egg shells gently on a hard surface but do not remove the shells. The purpose is to crack the entire surface of the egg shells in a network of fine lines.
5. Combine 1½ cups cold water for 5 eggs or 2 cups for 10 eggs, the teabags, salt, soy sauce and five-spice powder in the saucepan. Arrange the cracked eggs in the saucepan.
6. Place the saucepan over low heat and cook for 45 minutes. Remove the pan from the heat and let the eggs stand until completely cold.
7. Peel the eggs carefully. Cut the eggs into halves lengthwise and arrange with the white sides up to show the marble patterns on a platter lined with vegetable greens.

YIELD: *6 servings.* **Nutritional Facts Per Serving:** Calories 80; Total Fat 5g (Saturated Fat 1.5g); Cholesterol 210mg; Sodium 260mg; Total Carbohydrate 1g (Dietary Fiber 0g; Sugars 0g); Protein 6g

Shao-Mai
(A Kind of Dim-Sum) *(photo: page 70)*

Dim-sum means snack in Chinese. Shao-Mai is a very elegant snack for both its appearance and its excellent taste. It is served with a dipping sauce and hot Chinese tea.

Ingredients:

Garnishes:
3 tablespoons dried black mushrooms
3 tablespoons cooked green peas
3 tablespoons finely diced cooked ham
3 tablespoons finely diced cooked shrimp

Dough:
1 cup all-purpose flour
1 cup cake flour
1/2 cup hot water
1 egg, beaten

Filling:
12 ounces ground pork
1 tablespoon soy sauce
1/2 teaspoon salt
1 1/2 teaspoons rice wine
1/4 teaspoon black pepper
1/4 teaspoon sugar
1/2 cup finely shredded bamboo shoots
1 tablespoon sesame oil
1 tablespoon cornstarch

Dipping Sauce:
1 tablespoon Hoisin sauce
1 teaspoon soy sauce
1 teaspoon sesame oil

Preparation:

- Soak the dried black mushrooms in boiling water for 15 minutes. Drain, squeeze dry, discard the stems and chop the caps finely to yield 3 tablespoons. Assemble the mushrooms, peas, ham and shrimp separately to be used for garnish and set aside.
- Prepare the Dough by combining the all-purpose and cake flour in a bowl. Add the hot water and mix well with chopsticks. Add the egg and mix well. Knead the dough in the bowl until smooth. Cover the bowl with a moist cloth to prevent drying while preparing the filling.
- Prepare the Filling by combining the pork, soy sauce, salt, rice wine, pepper, sugar, bamboo shoots, sesame oil and cornstarch in a bowl, mix well and set the Filling aside.
- Blend the Hoisin sauce with 1 teaspoon soy sauce and 1 teaspoon sesame oil in a small dish and set aside to serve with the Shao-Mai as a Dipping Sauce.

Procedure:

1. Turn the Dough onto a surface lightly sprinkled with cornstarch and knead lightly. Divide into 30 small pieces and roll each piece into a 2-inch diameter circle.
2. Place about 1 tablespoon of the prepared pork Filling in the center of each circle. Bring opposite sides of the circle to the center and pinch to secure. Bring the remaining opposite sides to the center and pinch. The result should resemble a four-leaf clover when the pockets are opened. Garnish each of the clover leaves with 2 or 3 pieces of a single prepared garnish.
3. Arrange the Shao-Mai in a steamer lined with a single layer of damp oiled cheesecloth. Steam for 20 minutes.
4. Remove to a serving platter and serve immediately with the prepared Dipping Sauce or plum sauce.

YIELD: *6 servings.* **Nutritional Facts Per Serving:** Calories 230; Total Fat 6g (Saturated Fat 1.5g); Cholesterol 50mg; Sodium 300mg; Total Carbohydrate 24g (Dietary Fiber 2g; Sugars 0g); Protein 19g

Pork Ribs with Dried Fermented Black Beans

Dried fermented black beans are described in the Hunan Level and can be purchased in Asian food markets.

Ingredients:

1 1/3 pounds pork spareribs
3 tablespoons dried fermented
    black beans
1 tablespoon crushed garlic
1 tablespoon minced green bell pepper
2 slices fresh gingerroot, minced
1 tablespoon rice wine or pale
    dry sherry
2 tablespoons soy sauce
1 1/2 teaspoons sugar
1/4 cup plum sauce
2 tablespoons peanut or vegetable oil

Preparation:

- Cut the spareribs into thirty 1-inch pieces and set aside.
- Rinse the dried fermented black beans lightly and drain. Combine the beans with the garlic, bell pepper and gingerroot in a small dish and set aside.
- Combine the rice wine, soy sauce, sugar and plum sauce in a small bowl, mix well and set aside.

Procedure:

1. Preheat a wok. Add the peanut oil and the black fermented bean mixture and stir-fry over medium heat for several seconds.
2. Increase the heat to high. Add the spareribs and stir-fry just once.
3. Add the plum sauce mixture and stir-fry until the ribs are coated with the mixture.
4. Remove the ribs and sauce to a heatproof dish. Place the dish in a steamer and steam for 40 minutes.
5. Serve the ribs immediately with Steamed White Rice (page 26).

YIELD: *6 servings.* **Nutritional Facts Per Serving:** Calories 350; Total Fat 28g (Saturated Fat 9g); Cholesterol 80mg; Sodium 460mg; Total Carbohydrate 6g (Dietary Fiber 0g; Sugars 1g); Protein 18g

This popular Dim-sum is often served at lunch time in Chinese restaurants. The meat becomes well-flavored and very tender after long steaming.

Steamed Meat Pao (Northern Cuisine)
(Snow-White Fluffy Meat Buns) *(photo: page 70)*

Steamed buns are a popular dim-sum that can be a complete meal when served with soup. The most difficult part of the recipe is the dough which requires practice and time. The buns could be made ahead, frozen, and resteamed for 15 minutes before serving.

For the Dough

Ingredients:

1 envelope dry yeast
$\frac{1}{4}$ cup (105- to 115-degree) warm water
$\frac{3}{4}$ cup warm milk
$\frac{1}{4}$ cup peanut oil
$4\frac{1}{2}$ tablespoons sugar
$\frac{1}{2}$ teaspoon salt
$3\frac{1}{2}$ to 4 cups cake or all-purpose flour
$\frac{1}{2}$ teaspoon vegetable oil

Preparation:

- Dissolve the yeast in the warm water in a bowl. Let stand for about 3 minutes.
- Blend the milk, peanut oil, sugar and salt together in a small bowl. Add the dissolved yeast and mix well.
- Place $3\frac{1}{2}$ cups of the flour in a large bowl. Add the milk mixture and mix well. Knead in enough additional flour gradually to make a smooth firm dough. Brush the surface with the $\frac{1}{2}$ teaspoon oil, cover with a moist cloth and let rise in a warm place for $1\frac{1}{2}$ hours.
- Punch the dough down and let rest for several minutes. Turn the dough onto a lightly floured surface and knead lightly. Place the dough in a greased bowl, turning to coat the surface, cover with a moist cloth and let rise in a warm place for $1\frac{1}{2}$ hours or until doubled in bulk.

Pao can also be filled with sweet red bean paste and served as a dessert. The meat filling can be varied to use roast or ground pork or a mixture of pork and shrimp.

For the Filling

Ingredients:

    3 large dried black mushrooms
    1 pound lean pork
    1 tablespoon cornstarch
    1 tablespoon soy sauce
    1 tablespoon rice wine or pale
        dry sherry
    2 tablespoons peanut or vegetable oil
    1/4 cup chopped onion
    1/4 cup diced bamboo shoots
    1/4 cup diced water chestnuts
    2 tablespoons Hoisin sauce
    2 teaspoons sugar
    Salt and black pepper to taste

Preparation:

- Soak the mushrooms in boiling water to cover for 15 minutes. Drain and squeeze dry, discard the stems and dice.
- Dice the pork into small cubes and place in a bowl. Add the cornstarch, soy sauce and sherry and mix until coated.
- Preheat a wok. Add the peanut oil and onion and stir-fry until the onion is beginning to turn brown.
- Add the pork and stir-fry until the pork changes color. Add the mushrooms, bamboo shoots and water chestnuts and stir-fry for several seconds.
- Add the Hoisin sauce, sugar, salt and pepper and stir-fry until well mixed. Remove the pork mixture to a bowl and let stand until cool.

Assemble:

1. Divide the dough into 2 portions. Knead each portion on a lightly floured surface and shape into a 1-inch diameter log. Cut each log into 12 portions.
2. Roll each dough piece into a small circle. Spoon 1 tablespoon of the pork filling into the center of the circle, bring the dough up to enclose the filling, pleating and twisting to seal at the top. Place the bun on a 2-inch square of waxed paper.
3. Repeat with the remaining dough and filling.
4. Arrange the buns on the waxed paper squares in a steamer. Steam for 15 to 20 minutes. Serve immediately.

YIELD: *8 servings.* **Nutritional Facts Per Serving:** Calories 410; Total Fat 15g (Saturated Fat 3g); Cholesterol 40mg; Sodium 330mg; Total Carbohydrate 51g (Dietary Fiber 1g; Sugars 10g); Protein 18g

Kung Pao Chicken Ding (Szechuan Cuisine) (Diced Chicken with Dried Red Pepper) *(photo: page 71)*

Ingredients:

1 pound chicken breasts

Marinade:

1 tablespoon light soy sauce
1 teaspoon rice wine
4$^1/_2$ teaspoons cornstarch

6 to 8 dried red peppers

Seasoning Sauce:

1 tablespoon dark soy sauce
1 teaspoon hot bean sauce
1 teaspoon Hoisin sauce
1 teaspoon rice wine or pale dry sherry
1 teaspoon rice vinegar
1 teaspoon sesame oil
1 teaspoon sugar
1 teaspoon cornstarch
$^1/_2$ teaspoon salt

5 cups peanut or soybean oil for deep-frying
2 tablespoons peanut or other vegetable oil
1 teaspoon chopped fresh gingerroot
$^1/_2$ cup skinless peanuts

Preparation:

- Discard the skin and bones from the chicken and cut into $^1/_2$-inch cubes. Pound the cubes lightly with the back of the cleaver and place the chicken cubes in a bowl.
- Mix the 1 tablespoon light soy sauce, 1 teaspoon rice wine and 4$^1/_2$ teaspoons cornstarch together, pour over the chicken cubes and mix until coated. Marinate the chicken in the refrigerator for 20 minutes.
- Wipe the red peppers with a moist paper towel, discard the stems, tips and seeds, cut the peppers into $^1/_2$ inch long pieces and set aside.
- Combine the 1 tablespoon dark soy sauce, hot bean sauce, Hoisin sauce, 1 teaspoon rice wine, rice vinegar, sesame oil, sugar, 1 teaspoon cornstarch and salt in a small dish, mix well and set the Seasoning Sauce aside.

Procedure:

1. Heat the peanut oil to 350 to 375 degrees in a wok or deep fryer. Add several pieces of chicken at a time; do not crowd. Deep-fry for 30 seconds and remove to drain on paper towels.
2. Preheat a wok. Add 2 tablespoons oil and the dried red pepper. Stir-fry until the peppers are black.
3. Add the gingerroot and the chicken and stir-fry for several seconds.
4. Add the prepared Seasoning Sauce and cook until the sauce thickens, stirring constantly.
5. Stir in the peanuts and serve immediately.

YIELD: *6 servings.* **Nutritional Facts Per Serving:** Calories 240; Total Fat 14g (Saturated Fat 2.5g); Cholesterol 45mg; Sodium 430mg; Total Carbohydrate 7g (Dietary Fiber 1g; Sugars 1g); Protein 21g

One of the most popular Chinese restaurant dishes originated when Kung Pao, a palace guard who loved cooking, overcooked red peppers in hot oil. The exciting taste in the oil flavored the chicken and peanuts. This pleased the emperor, who promoted Kung Pao to high office.

The Chinese feel that a man who can cook shows a sign of intelligence.

Assorted Three-Shreds Cold Plate (Eastern Cuisine) *(photo: page 71)*

This dish features the contrast of three distinct colors as well as the fine technique of Chinese shred cutting. Try varying the shredded ingredients with hard-cooked egg, bean sprouts, jellyfish or other colorful contrasts. It is a wonderful, cool salad.

Light soy sauce is made from rare white soybeans. The light color is preferred for light meats, chicken, fish and other seafood so the food has better visual appeal.

Ingredients:

Sauce:
2 tablespoons light soy sauce
3 tablespoons rice vinegar
2 teaspoons sesame oil
1 tablespoon sugar

5 to 6 ounces cooked ham
1 small cucumber
Salt
1 egg
1 tablespoon vegetable oil
3 cups water
1 (4-ounce) package bean threads

Preparation:

- Combine the light soy sauce, rice vinegar, sesame oil and sugar in a small bowl and mix well. Refrigerate the Sauce so that when it is added just before serving the ingredients will retain their colorful appearance.
- Cut the cooked ham into thin 2-inch shreds and set aside.
- Peel off only the bumpy, rough spots of the cucumber. Rub the cucumber with salt, rinse, drain and pat dry. Discard the ends and cut diagonally into 2-inch lengths. Cut the cucumber into shreds the same size as the ham and set aside.
- Beat the egg well and add a pinch of salt. Heat a wok with 1 tablespoon vegetable oil. Add the egg all at once and swirl the wok to spread the egg thinly over the surface. Cook for several seconds until firm, turn the egg over and almost immediately remove to a cutting board. Cut the egg into shreds that match the ham and cucumber in size and set aside.

Procedure:

1. Bring 3 cups water to a boil in a saucepan. Add the bean threads and press to immerse completely. Turn the heat off and let stand for 5 minutes or until the bean threads are soft and transparent. Drain the bean threads and plunge into cold water to chill and stop the cooking.
2. Drain the bean threads and cut into 2-inch lengths.
3. Spread the bean threads evenly over the bottom of a serving platter. Mentally divide the bean thread-covered platter into thirds and mound one portion with ham shreds, one with cucumber shreds, and one with egg shreds.
4. Drizzle the chilled Sauce over the top just before serving.

YIELD: *4 servings.* **Nutritional Facts Per Serving:** Calories 150; Total Fat 10g (Saturated Fat 2g); Cholesterol 75mg; Sodium 1000mg; Total Carbohydrate 7g (Dietary Fiber 1g; Sugars 5g); Protein 10g

Prawns on Toast
(Taiwanese Dim-Sum) *(photo: page 71)*

Ingredients:

- 1½ pounds prawns
- 2 slices fresh gingerroot
- 2 green onions
- Dash of black pepper
- ½ teaspoon salt
- 1 teaspoon rice wine
- 6 slices bread
- 4 egg whites
- 2 tablespoons flour
- 1 tablespoons cornstarch
- 6 cups peanut or vegetable oil for deep-frying
- 1 teaspoon minced ham
- ½ teaspoon black sesame seeds
- 24 leaves coriander or Chinese parsley

Preparation:

- Peel the prawns leaving the tails. Butterfly-cut the prawns and pound lightly with the cleaver. Rinse the prawns and pat dry.
- Mince the gingerroot and green onions and combine with the pepper, salt and rice wine. Coat the prawns with the mixture and let stand for 20 minutes.
- Toast the bread lightly (or use day-old bread) and remove the crusts. Cut each slice into halves and set aside.
- Beat the egg whites in a mixing bowl for 5 minutes or until very dry stiff peaks form. Mix the flour and cornstarch together and fold the mixture into the egg whites.

Procedure:

1. Pat the prawns dry. Spread the egg white mixture evenly on the toast pieces, place a prawn on the toast with the tail up.
2. Cover the prawn with additional egg white mixture and sprinkle with ham and black sesame seeds. Add a coriander leaf in the center.
3. Preheat the oil for deep-frying to 350 to 375 degrees in a deep fryer.
4. Hold the prepared toast with the shrimp side up and slide into the hot oil carefully; do not crowd. Cook for a few seconds and turn the toast over with the shrimp side down.
5. Deep-fry for 2 minutes, drain on paper towels and serve immediately.

To butterfly-cut the prawns is to open the body into two equal halves to resemble a butterfly. Insert the knife or cleaver into the prawn at the tail and cut the length of the shrimp to, but not through the other side, following the curve, and open carefully.

YIELD: *6 servings.* **Nutritional Facts Per Serving:** Calories 450; Total Fat 13g (Saturated Fat 2g); Cholesterol 115mg; Sodium 350mg; Total Carbohydrate 55g (Dietary Fiber 2g; Sugars 0g); Protein 27g

Szechuan Cabbage, Pork and Bean Thread Soup (Szechuan Cuisine)

Ingredients:

¼ cup pork loin
1 teaspoon soy sauce
1 teaspoon cornstarch
1 ounce bean threads
3 cups water
1 teaspoon salt
½ teaspoon sugar
2 tablespoons Szechuan cabbage
½ cup thinly sliced cucumber
1 tablespoon chopped green onion
Dash of black pepper
½ teaspoon sesame oil
¼ teaspoon soy sauce
2 tablespoons peanut or vegetable oil

Preparation:

- Cut the pork into thin shreds about 1 inch long and place in a bowl. Mix the 1 teaspoon soy sauce and cornstarch together, add to the pork, mix until coated and set aside.
- Place the bean threads in a bowl and cover with boiling water. Let stand for 5 minutes and drain well.
- Combine the 3 cups water, salt and sugar, mix until the salt and sugar dissolve and set aside.
- Rinse the Szechuan cabbage to remove the excessive salt and red chili powder. Cut the Szechuan cabbage and the cucumbers into thin shreds about 1 inch long and set aside.
- Combine the green onion, pepper, sesame oil and ¼ teaspoon soy sauce in a small dish and set aside.

Procedure:

1. Preheat a wok. Add the peanut oil and the pork and stir-fry for several seconds and remove the pork.
2. Pour the water mixture into the wok and heat until boiling. Add the Szechuan cabbage, cucumber, bean threads and the pork and mix well.
3. Bring the mixture to a boil, stir in the green onion mixture and serve immediately.

YIELD: *4 servings.* **Nutritional Facts Per Serving:** Calories 100; Total Fat 9g (Saturated Fat 1g); Cholesterol 10mg; Sodium 700mg; Total Carbohydrate 2g (Dietary Fiber 0g; Sugars 1g); Protein 3g

Basic

Shredded Beef with Green Pepper (p. 27)

Egg Drop Soup (p. 28)

Chicken with Cashew Nuts (p. 29)

Sweet and Sour Pork (p. 30)

Basic

Almond Float (p. 31)

Wonton Soup (p. 32); Fried Wontons (p. 33)

Egg Rolls (p. 34)

Fried Rice (p. 35)

Advanced

Egg Foo Yung (p. 39)

Clear Steamed Fish (p. 40)

Cantonese Barbecue Roast Pork (p. 41)

Roast Pork Lo-Mein (p. 42)

Advanced

Genghis Khan Barbecue (p. 43)

Chiao-Tzu Northern Dumplings (p. 44)

Mandarin Thin Pancakes (p. 46)

Moo Shi Pork (p. 47)

Gourmet I

Lemon Chicken (p. 49)

Pearl Balls (p. 51)

Four Kinds of Braised Vegetables (p. 52)

Paper-Wrapped Chicken (p. 53)

Gourmet I

Hot and Sour Soup *(p. 54)*

Marble Eggs *(p. 55)*

Shao-Mai *(p. 56)*

Steamed Meat Pao *(p. 58)*

Gourmet II

Kung Pao Chicken Ding (p. 61)

Assorted Three-Shreds Cold Plate (p. 62)

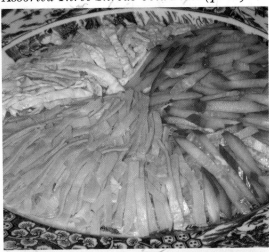

Prawns on Toast (p. 63)

Lobster Cantonese (p. 82)

Gourmet II

Sweet and Sour Fish (p. 83)

Traditional Chinese Tamales (p. 84)

Sliced Beef in Curry Sauce (p. 85)

Eight-Jewel Chicken (p. 86)

Gourmet III

Eight-Treasures Rice Pudding (p. 89)

Taiwanese Fried Pork Meatballs (p. 90)

Shrimp in Sour Sauce (p. 92)

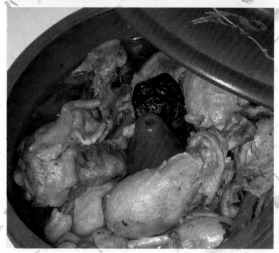

Sesame Chicken in Yunnan Pot (p. 95)

Gourmet III

Chinese Almond Cookies (p. 97)

Northern Cha-Chian Mein (p. 99)

Dragon Phoenix Paradise (p. 100)

Maki-Zushi (p. 103)

Szechuan Cuisine

Shredded Beef with Yu-Xiang Sauce (p. 114)

Hot and Spicy Fried Crabs (p. 115)

Mongolian Lamb (p. 116)

Twice-Cooked Pork (p. 119)

Szechuan Cuisine

Eggplant Szechuan-Style (p. 120)

Fragrant Crispy Duck (p. 124)

Dan-Dan Mein (p. 150)

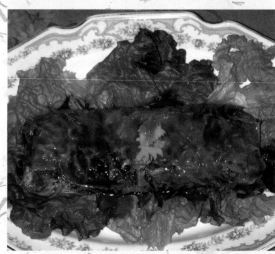

Vegetarian Fish in Hot Bean Sauce (p. 154)

Hunan Cuisine

Dry-Fried String Beans (p. 131)

Shark's Fin Soup (p. 132)

Lovers Shrimp (p. 134)

Dry-Fried Shredded Beef (p. 135)

Hunan Cuisine

Honey-Glazed Ham (p. 136)

Minced Chicken in Lettuce Bowls (p. 137)

Chinese Onion Cake (p. 138)

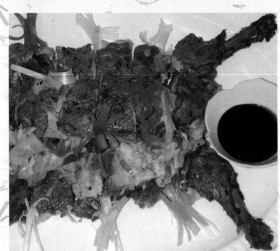

Tea-Smoked Duck (p. 140)

Vegetarian Cuisine

Vegetarian Steak (p. 152)

Stuffed Bean Curd in Brown Sauce (p. 153)

Nori-Maki Sushi (p. 156)

Braised Yellow Partridge (p. 157)

Vegetarian Cuisine

Five-Fragrant Pressed Tofu (p. 158)

Sesame Glutinous Rice Balls (p. 159)

Arhat's Feast (p. 160)

Steamed Acorn Squash Bowls (p. 161)

Sea Scallops and Quail Eggs with Assorted Vegetables (Eastern Cuisine)

Quail eggs and baby corn (miniature corn on the cob) can be found in the canned food section of Asian markets. Abalone (canned) may be substituted for the sea scallops. Slice into thin round pieces and cut off the edges.

Ingredients:

4 dried black mushrooms
1 pound sea scallops

Marinade:
1 tablespoon light soy sauce
1½ tablespoons rice wine
1½ teaspoons cornstarch

4 thin slices carrot
16 (½ × 1½-inch) pieces Chinese cabbage
½ cup snowpeas or green peas
16 (1½-inch) baby corn
16 quail eggs
1 tablespoon cornstarch
2 tablespoons water
Peanut oil for deep-frying
1 tablespoon peanut or vegetable oil
1½ cups chicken stock
Several drops of sesame oil
Dash of black pepper

Preparation:

- Soak the mushrooms in boiling water to cover for about 15 minutes. Drain the mushrooms, cut off and discard the stems, slice the caps thinly and set aside.
- Cut the sea scallops into halves. Marinate in a mixture of the light soy sauce, rice wine and cornstarch for 10 minutes.
- Cut each of the carrot slices into a butterfly shape and set aside.
- Cut the Chinese cabbage into specified-size pieces. Pinch the ends from the snowpeas and discard the strings. Cut the baby corn into halves lengthwise.
- Drain the quail eggs and set aside.
- Dissolve the cornstarch in the 2 tablespoons water and set aside.

Procedure:

1. Deep-fry the scallops in 375-degree oil for 2 minutes and drain on paper towels in a colander.
2. Preheat a wok. Add the 1 tablespoon peanut oil and the mushrooms and stir-fry for several seconds and add the chicken stock, cabbage, baby corn and snowpeas.
3. Bring the soup to a boil and add the quail eggs and the carrot.
4. Stir in the cornstarch mixture and cook until thickened, stirring constantly.
5. Add the deep-fried scallops and stir several times while heating.
6. Stir in the sesame oil and pepper and serve immediately.

YIELD: *6 servings.* **Nutritional Facts Per Serving:** Calories 180; Total Fat 6g (Saturated Fat 1.5g); Cholesterol 230mg; Sodium 360mg; Total Carbohydrate 11g (Dietary Fiber 1g; Sugars 1g); Protein 19g

Lobster Cantonese (Tsao Lung Ha) *(photo: page 71)*

Ingredients:

1 (1½- to 2-pound) live lobster
1 tablespoon fermented black beans
White of 1 scallion
1 tablespoon cornstarch
2 tablespoons water
1 egg
2 tablespoons peanut, corn or
    vegetable oil
1 garlic clove, crushed
2 slices fresh gingerroot, minced
4 ounces lean ground pork
1 tablespoon soy sauce
1 tablespoon rice wine or pale
    dry sherry
½ teaspoon sugar
Dash of black pepper
1 cup water

Preparation:

- Rinse the lobster and use the cleaver to cut off the tail, claws and legs. Discard the head shell, feelers, white gills and stomach and intestines. Crack the claws and legs and split the lobster lengthwise using the cleaver. Cut the lobster meat into 1-inch cubes and set aside.
- Mash the black beans with the flat side of the cleaver and set aside.
- Rinse the scallion, pat dry, cut into ¼-inch dice and set aside.
- Dissolve the cornstarch in 2 tablespoons water and set aside.
- Beat the egg in a small dish and set aside.

Procedure:

1. Preheat a wok over high heat. Add the peanut oil, scallion, garlic, gingerroot and black beans and stir-fry until the scallion is light brown.
2. Add the ground pork and salt and stir-fry until the pork is no longer pink.
3. Add the lobster, soy sauce, rice wine, sugar and pepper and mix well. Stir-fry for several seconds.
4. Pour 1 cup water into the wok, cover and bring to a boil.
5. Stir in the cornstarch mixture and cook until thickened, stirring constantly.
6. Turn the heat off and drip the beaten egg through two cooking chopsticks, stirring in circles gently just once with the chopsticks. Serve immediately.

YIELD: *6 servings.* **Nutritional Facts Per Serving:** Calories 220; Total Fat 11g (Saturated Fat 2.5g); Cholesterol 155mg; Sodium 720mg; Total Carbohydrate 3g (Dietary Fiber 0g; Sugars 0g); Protein 26g

Sweet and Sour Fish
(Taiwanese Cuisine) *(photo: page 72)*

Ingredients:

1 (1½-pound) fish

Marinade:

1 tablespoon rice wine or pale dry
    sherry
2 (2-inch pieces) green onion,
    shredded
2 slices fresh gingerroot, minced
1 teaspoon salt
Dash of black pepper

2 tablespoons cornstarch
2 tablespoons water
⅓ cup all-purpose flour

Sweet and Sour Sauce:

¼ cup sugar
¼ cup rice vinegar
¼ cup ketchup
¼ cup water
1 tablespoon light soy sauce
1 tablespoon cornstarch
½ teaspoon salt

6 cups peanut or vegetable oil for
    deep-frying
2 tablespoons peanut or vegetable oil
1 garlic clove, crushed
½ cup shredded onion
½ cup shredded green bell pepper

Garnishes:

2 tablespoons shredded green onions
1 tablespoon shredded fresh gingerroot
1½ teaspoons shredded hot red pepper
    (optional)
2 tablespoons coriander

Preparation:

- Scale and gut the fish, leaving the head and tail intact. Make diagonal slices in the fish on both sides, cutting almost to the bone.
- Prepare the Marinade by mixing 1 tablespoon rice wine, green onion and gingerroot, 1 teaspoon salt and a dash of pepper. Spread the Marinade over both sides of the fish and let stand for 20 minutes.
- Blend 2 tablespoons cornstarch with 2 tablespoons water. Spread the mixture over the inside and outside of the fish. Coat the outside of the fish with the flour.
- Prepare the Sweet and Sour Sauce by blending the sugar, ¼ cup rice vinegar, ketchup, ¼ cup water, light soy sauce, 1 tablespoon cornstarch and ½ teaspoon salt in a small bowl and set aside.

Procedure:

1. Preheat the oil for deep-frying to 350 to 375 degrees in a large wok or deep fryer. Hold the fish by the tail and slip carefully into the hot oil. Deep-fry for 5 to 6 minutes, drain and place on a serving platter.
2. Heat the 2 tablespoons peanut oil in a wok, add the garlic and shredded onion and stir-fry for several seconds. Add the green pepper and Sweet and Sour Sauce and mix well. Bring the mixture to a boil and pour over the fish on the serving platter.
3. Sprinkle the garnishes over the top to decorate and serve immediately.

YIELD: *5 servings.* **Nutritional Facts Per Serving:** Calories 250; Total Fat 17g (Saturated Fat 2.5g); Cholesterol 0mg; Sodium 270mg; Total Carbohydrate 25g (Dietary Fiber 1g; Sugars 11g); Protein 1g

Traditional Chinese Tamales (Dim-Sum) *(photo: page 72)*

Dried bamboo leaves are sold in packages at Chinese markets. For this recipe, the leaves need to be about 18 inches long and 3 inches wide.

Chinese tamales for the Feast of May 5th (fifth day of the fifth month of the lunar calendar) are as traditional as turkey for the American Thanksgiving. Historically the day commemorates Chen-Yuen, a great statesman, who took his own life (295 B.C.) when his democratic ideas angered the emperor.

Ingredients:

1 1/2 cups glutinous rice
8 ounces lean pork loin
1 garlic clove
1 scallion
1 tablespoon soy sauce
1 tablespoon rice wine or pale
   dry sherry
1 teaspoon sesame oil
Pinch of salt
1 teaspoon sugar
1/4 teaspoon five-spice powder
18 dried bamboo leaves
1/2 cup boiling water
6 dried mushrooms
12 dried shrimp
1/4 cup whole bamboo shoots

Preparation:

- Soak the glutinous rice in cold water to cover overnight.
- Cut the pork loin into 1-cubes and place in a bowl.
- Bruise the garlic with the flat side of a cleaver. Cut the scallion into 2-inch pieces and then dice into small pieces.
- Combine the soy sauce, rice wine, sesame oil, salt, sugar, five-spice powder, garlic and scallion in a small bowl and mix well. Pour over the pork and marinate for 30 minutes.
- Soak the bamboo leaves in cold water to cover for 30 minutes or longer.
- Pour the boiling water over the mushrooms in a small bowl and let stand for 15 minutes; drain.
- Squeeze the mushrooms dry. Cut the mushrooms into halves or thirds and set aside.
- Soak the shrimp in 1/2 cup cold water for 15 minutes.
- Dice the bamboo shoots into 1/4-inch cubes.

Procedure:

1. Place 3 bamboo leaves together with the sides slightly overlapping and shape into a funnel. Pack the rice tightly into the bottom one-third of the funnel. Add the desired amount of the marinated pork, 2 shrimp, mushroom slices and bamboo cubes and press additional rice on top to almost fill the bamboo leaf funnel. Fold the bamboo leaves over to form a triangular package and secure with string. Repeat with the remaining ingredients.

2. Bring a generous amount of water to a boil in a wok. Add the tamales, cover the wok and boil for 30 minutes.

3. Remove the tamales, drain, untie the string and open the bamboo leaves carefully.

Presentation:

- Serve the tamales with tea, or place in a bowl with 1/2 cup boiling soup stock, or serve with a dipping sauce made of Hoisin sauce, light soy sauce and sesame oil.

YIELD: *6 tamales.* **Nutritional Facts Per Tamale:** Calories 260; Total Fat 4g (Saturated Fat 1.5g); Cholesterol 25g; Sodium 220mg; Total Carbohydrate 43g (Dietary Fiber 2g; Sugars 1g); Protein 12g

Sliced Beef in Curry Sauce (South-Western Cuisine) *(photo: page 72)*

Ingredients:

8 ounces lean flank or top round steak

Marinade:

1 tablespoon soy sauce
1½ teaspoons cornstarch
1 teaspoon sugar
1 tablespoon cold water

1 tablespoon peanut or vegetable oil
1 pound potatoes
1 or 2 carrots
2 tablespoons peanut or vegetable oil
1 cup diced onion
4½ teaspoons curry powder
1½ cups cold water
1½ teaspoons salt
1 teaspoon sugar
1 tablespoon peanut or vegetable oil

Preparation:

- Cut the steak across the grain into thin 1-inch squares and place in a bowl. Mix 1 tablespoon soy sauce, cornstarch, 1 teaspoon sugar and 1 tablespoon water together and add to the steak, stirring to coat. Drizzle with 1 tablespoon peanut oil to prevent drying but do not stir. Marinate for 30 minutes.
- Peel the potatoes, cut into diagonal slices and set aside.
- Roll and cut enough of the carrots to yield 20 slices. (See Cutting Techniques on page 18.)

Procedure:

1. Heat 2 tablespoons peanut oil in a wok over high heat and add the onion. Stir-fry for several seconds.
2. Add the potatoes and carrots and stir-fry for 30 seconds. Add the curry powder, 1½ cups water, salt and sugar and mix well. Reduce the heat to medium, cover and cook for 10 to 15 minutes.
3. Arrange the steak slices evenly over the vegetables in the wok. Increase the heat to high and cover tightly.
4. Cook for a few minutes or just until the vegetables are tender-crisp and the steak is done to taste. Turn the heat off. Serve immediately.

YIELD: *6 servings.* **Nutritional Facts Per Serving:** Calories 210; Total Fat 10g (Saturated Fat 2g); Cholesterol 20mg; Sodium 790mg; Total Carbohydrate 21g (Dietary Fiber 3g; Sugars 4g); Protein 10g

Eight-Jewel Chicken *(photo: page 72)*

This is a famous and highly celebrated banquet dish for special occasions. Be sure to use original and authentic ingredients. Lotus seeds resemble macadamia nuts and have been boiled with sugar and water. Lotus nuts, as well as, gingko nuts can be found in Asian markets. Star anise, also found in Asian markets, is described in the Hunan Level.

Ingredients:

1 (4½-pound) roasting chicken
Eight-Jewel Stuffing (page 87)
2 tablespoons soy sauce
¼ cup cornstarch
6 cups (about) peanut or vegetable oil
    for deep-frying
Whites of 2 green onions, chopped
2 slices fresh gingerroot, minced
1 star anise
1 tablespoon rice wine or pale
    dry sherry
2 tablespoons soy sauce
1½ teaspoons sugar
2 cups water
Lettuce leaves

Preparation:

- Debone the chicken using kitchen scissors, being careful to leave the chicken skin intact. Reserve the carcass to use in making soup stock.
- Pack the cooled Eight-Jewel Stuffing into the boned chicken carefully to avoid tearing the flesh and skin. Sew up the neck and bottom cavity openings.
- Rub the outside of the stuffed chicken with 2 tablespoons soy sauce and sprinkle with the ¼ cup cornstarch to cover well.

Procedure:

1. Deep-fry the chicken in hot oil over high heat until golden brown. Drain the chicken and mold as necessary to resemble the original shape.
2. Layer the chopped green onions evenly in the bottom of a deep skillet or other pan. Place the chicken on the bed of green onions and add the gingerroot, star anise, 1 tablespoon rice wine, 2 tablespoon soy sauce, sugar and 2 cups water.
3. Cook, covered, over medium heat for 25 minutes or until the liquid has evaporated.

Presentation:

- Remove the chicken to a serving platter. Garnish the platter by surrounding the chicken with lettuce leaves.
- Cut the chicken into halves lengthwise and then make 3 cuts across the chicken to make a total of 8 pieces. Serve immediately.

Eight-Jewel Stuffing

Ingredients:

- 1 cup glutinous rice
- 4 dried black mushrooms
- 1 scallion
- 1 tablespoon soy sauce
- 1 tablespoon rice wine or pale dry sherry
- $1/2$ teaspoon salt
- 1 tablespoon peanut or vegetable oil
- $1/2$ cup shredded pork
- Giblets of the roasting chicken, shredded
- 5 dried shrimp
- $1/4$ cup shredded bamboo shoots
- $1/4$ cup green peas, lotus seeds or canned whole gingko nuts

Preparation:

- Soak the rice in cold water to cover for 7 hours to overnight.
- Soak the black mushrooms in boiling water to cover for 15 minutes, drain, discard the stems, shred the caps and set aside.
- Cut the scallion into $1/4$-inch dice.
- Combine the soy sauce, rice wine and salt in a small dish and set aside.

Procedure:

1. Heat the 1 tablespoon peanut oil in a wok. Add the diced scallion, shredded pork and chicken giblets and stir-fry until no longer pink.
2. Add the shrimp, bamboo shoots, mushrooms and the soy sauce mixture and stir-fry for several seconds.
3. Add the peas and the glutinous rice and stir-fry for several seconds. Remove the mixture from the wok and let stand until cool.

YIELD: *10 servings.* **Nutritional Facts Per Serving:** Calories 370; Total Fat 22g (Saturated Fat 5g); Cholesterol 75mg; Sodium 500mg; Total Carbohydrate 21g (Dietary Fiber 1g; Sugars 0g); Protein 20g

If you desire to serve the chicken with a sauce, increase the amount of water in Step #2 (page 86) from 2 cups to 4 cups. The cooking time should be increased from 25 minutes to 1 hour and the water will not evaporate completely. Strain the cooking liquid into a small saucepan, stir in a mixture of $1^1/2$ teaspoons cornstarch and 1 tablespoon water and cook until thickened, stirring constantly. Pour the sauce over the chicken and serve immediately.

Eight-Treasures Rice Pudding (photo: page 73)

Ingredients:

10 red dates, pitted
Dried orange peel to taste
6 dried apricots
Prunes to taste
Raisins to taste
10 red or green maraschino cherries
1½ cups glutinous rice
1½ cups water
¼ cup sugar
¼ cup vegetable shortening
5 to 6 ounces sweet red bean paste

Almond Sauce:

1 cup water
1 tablespoon sugar
1 teaspoon almond extract
2 teaspoons cornstarch
2 teaspoons water

Preparation:

- Cut the dried fruits and cherries into thin slices and then into an assortment of shapes. Grease one large heatproof bowl or six small heatproof bowls. Arrange the prepared fruit in decorative patterns in the bottoms of the bowls and set aside.
- Place the rice in a bowl and add water to cover. Let the rice soak for 1 hour or longer before cooking.

Procedure:

1. Drain the soaking water off the rice. Combine the soaked rice and 1½ cups water in a saucepan. Bring to a boil over high heat, reduce the heat to low and cook for 10 minutes and remove from the heat.
2. Add ¼ cup sugar and the shortening to the hot rice and mix well.
3. Spoon half the rice mixture into the prepared bowls and press firmly. Spread the sweet bean paste over the rice and press firmly. Add the remaining rice, press firmly and even the top layer smoothly.
4. Place the bowls in a steamer and steam for 20 minutes.
5. Invert each bowl onto a plate to unmold.
6. Combine 1 cup water and 1 tablespoon sugar in a small saucepan. Bring to a boil over medium heat, stirring until the sugar dissolves. Add the almond extract to the sauce.
7. Blend the cornstarch with the 2 teaspoons water. Stir the cornstarch mixture into the hot mixture and cook until thickened, stirring constantly.
8. Spoon the Almond Sauce over the puddings. Let the puddings stand until cool.
9. The puddings may be prepared in advance, cooled, wrapped individually in plastic wrap and stored in the freezer. To serve, steam the unwrapped puddings in a steamer until heated through.

This is the most celebrated traditional dessert for serving at Chinese New Year banquets and wedding banquets.

YIELD: *6 servings.* **Nutritional Facts Per Serving:** Calories 360; Total Fat 9g (Saturated Fat 4g); Cholesterol 5mg; Sodium 10mg; Total Carbohydrate 64g (Dietary Fiber 2g; Sugars 18g); Protein 6g

Taiwanese Fried Pork Meatballs *(photo: page 73)*

Serve these meatballs as an appetizer or as a main dish with plain steamed rice. I am proud to share this recipe, one of my mother's.

Ingredients:

1 large tomato

Dipping Sauce:
2 tablespoons ketchup
1 teaspoon Hoisin sauce
1 teaspoon sesame chili oil

1 pound ground pork
1 egg, beaten
1 tablespoon dark soy sauce
1 tablespoon rice wine or pale
    dry sherry
1 tablespoon minced onion
1 teaspoon minced water chestnuts
1 teaspoon minced bamboo shoots
1 teaspoon minced fresh gingerroot
1 teaspoon sesame oil
1 tablespoon cornstarch
1/2 teaspoon sugar
1/4 teaspoon salt
Dash of black pepper
6 cups (about) peanut oil for
    deep-frying
6 soft green vegetable leaves

Preparation:

- Cut the core from the tomato and score the tomato into 8 wedges to but not through the bottom. Peel the skin of the wedges from the core about 1/3 of the length of the wedges and open carefully to resemble a flower's petals. Open the tomato enough to scoop out the seeds and pulp and invert on paper towels to drain.
- Prepare the Dipping Sauce for the meatballs by blending the ketchup, Hoisin sauce and sesame chili oil in a dish. Fill the hollowed tomato core with the Dipping Sauce.

Procedure:

1. Combine the ground pork, egg, soy sauce, rice wine, onion, water chestnuts, bamboo shoots, gingerroot, sesame oil, cornstarch, sugar, salt and pepper in a bowl. Mix with cooking chopsticks to start and then with fingers until very well mixed.
2. Preheat the peanut oil in a wok or tempura pan to 350 degrees.
3. Spoon the pork mixture into small portions by squeezing firmly in the palm of your left hand to shape into 1-inch balls. Add the meatballs to the hot oil carefully and deep-fry for 2 to 3 minutes or until cooked through and crisp. Drain on paper towels in a colander.

Presentation:

- Line the serving platter with the vegetable leaves. Place the prepared tomato, with the Dipping Sauce, in the center of the platter.
- Arrange the meatballs around the tomato and serve immediately. Dip each meatball into the sauce before eating.

YIELD: *6 servings.* **Nutritional Facts Per Serving:** Calories 310; Total Fat 27g (Saturated Fat 8g); Cholesterol 90mg; Sodium 320mg; Total Carbohydrate 2g (Dietary Fiber 0g; Sugars 0g); Protein 14g

Pon-Pon Chicken (Szechuan Cuisine) (Cold Shredded Chicken)

Ingredients:

Sauce:

1½ tablespoons sesame paste
1 tablespoon light soy sauce
1 tablespoon chili oil
1 teaspoon sugar
1 teaspoon bean sauce
1 teaspoon rice vinegar
1 teaspoon sesame oil
1 teaspoon minced green onion
½ teaspoon minced gingerroot
½ teaspoon minced garlic
¼ teaspoon finely crushed Szechuan
flower pepper

1 (2½-pound) chicken or 2 whole
chicken breasts
1 teaspoon salt

Preparation:

* Combine the sesame paste, light soy sauce, chili oil, sugar, bean sauce, rice vinegar and sesame oil in a dish and blend well. Add the green onion, gingerroot, garlic and flower pepper and mix well. Store the Sauce in a covered container in the refrigerator until serving time.

Procedure:

1. Place the chicken in a saucepan or wok. Add water to cover and the salt.
2. Bring to a boil over medium heat. Reduce the heat to a simmer and simmer for about 20 minutes or until the chicken is tender. Turn the heat off and let stand until cool.
3. Drain the chicken and reserve the broth for another purpose. Remove the meat from the bones and discard the skin and bones. Chill the chicken until serving time.
4. Cut the chicken into strips about ½ × 1½-inch and place in a bowl.
5. Stir the cold Sauce to mix well, add to the chicken and pon-pon (pon-pon means stirring to mix) until the chicken is coated with the sauce.
6. Arrange the chicken strips on a serving plate and garnish with fresh coriander or Chinese parsley leaves.

This dish is served as either an appetizer or a main dish. The interesting feature of this recipe is the rich sesame-flavored sauce which is a composite of seven tastes, making it uniquely Szechuan.

YIELD: *4 servings.* **Nutritional Facts Per Serving:** Calories 210; Total Fat 9g (Saturated Fat 1.5g); Cholesterol 65mg; Sodium 290mg; Total Carbohydrate 4g (Dietary Fiber 1g; Sugars 1g); Protein 28g

Shrimp in Sour Sauce (Szechuan Cuisine) *(photo: page 73)*

Ingredients:

1 pound fresh shrimp

Marinade:
1 teaspoon salt
1 teaspoon sesame oil
Dash of sugar
Dash of white pepper
1½ teaspoons cornstarch
1 egg white

2 egg yolks
3 tablespoons cornstarch
Whites of 2 green onions
2 red chili peppers, seeded
⅓ green bell pepper
2 slices fresh gingerroot, minced
3 garlic cloves, minced

Sauce:
2 tablespoons sugar
2 tablespoons rice vinegar
2 tablespoons water
3 tablespoons ketchup
1 teaspoon salt
1 teaspoon sesame oil

1 teaspoon cornstarch
1½ teaspoons water
6 cups (about) peanut or soybean oil
    for deep-frying
2 tablespoons vegetable oil
Top of 1 green onion, diced

Preparation:

- Peel the shrimp. Make slits lengthwise along the back deep enough to remove the veins, rinse and pat dry.
- Combine Marinade ingredients in a bowl and mix well. Dip the shrimp in the Marinade to coat, layer in a bowl and refrigerate.
- Beat the egg yolks, blend in 3 tablespoons cornstarch.
- Cut the whites of 2 green onions and the red chili peppers into ¼-inch dice. Discard the seeds and membranes from the green pepper and cut into ⅓-inch dice. Combine green onions, red chili peppers, green pepper, gingerroot and garlic in a small dish, mix well and set aside.
- Combine the Sauce ingredients in a small dish, mix well and set aside.
- Blend 1 teaspoon cornstarch with 1½ teaspoons water and set aside.

Procedure:

1. Stir the egg yolk mixture into the shrimp gently until the shrimp are coated.
2. Heat the 6 cups peanut oil to 375 degrees. Add the coated shrimp carefully one at a time to the hot oil using a tablespoon. Deep-fry for 2 minutes or until crisp and golden brown. Drain on paper towels in a colander.
3. Preheat a wok. Add 2 tablespoons vegetable oil and the green onion mixture. Stir-fry for several seconds.
4. Add the Sauce mixture and bring to a boil, stirring constantly.
5. Stir in the cornstarch and water mixture and cook until thickened, stirring constantly.
6. Place the shrimp on a serving platter and pour the sauce over the shrimp.
7. Sprinkle with the diced green onion top and serve immediately.

YIELD: *6 servings.* **Nutritional Facts Per Serving:** Calories 240; Total Fat 14g (Saturated Fat 2g); Cholesterol 175mg; Sodium 920mg; Total Carbohydrate 12g (Dietary Fiber 0g; Sugars 5g); Protein 17g

Stuffed Cabbage Chinese-Style (Northern Cuisine)

Ingredients:

1 (1½-pound) cabbage
Salt to taste

Stuffing:
12 ounces ground pork
¼ cup minced onion
2 slices fresh gingerroot, minced
1 tablespoon rice wine or pale
    dry sherry
1 tablespoon all-purpose flour
1 tablespoon cornstarch
1 egg, beaten
1 teaspoon salt

2 teaspoons cornstarch
2 tablespoons water
½ cup thinly sliced carrot
1 cup chicken broth

Preparation:

- Place the cabbage head upside down in a deep pot of boiling water. Let stand completely immersed for several minutes or until the cabbage leaves become soft. Drain the cabbage and remove the leaves carefully one at a time, trim the hard stems, flatten the leaves, sprinkle with salt and set aside.
- Prepare the Stuffing by combining the ground pork, onion, gingerroot, rice wine, flour, 1 tablespoon cornstarch, egg and 1 teaspoon salt in a bowl and mix well.
- Dissolve the 2 teaspoons cornstarch in the 2 tablespoons water and set aside.

Procedure:

1. Use about ⅓ of the cabbage leaves to line the bottom of a 2-quart heavy saucepan that has been lightly coated with sesame oil. Add a layer of half the carrot slices.
2. Spread half the Stuffing mixture into the pan and press evenly.
3. Repeat the layers of cabbage leaves, remaining carrot and the remaining Stuffing mixture.
4. Add a layer of the cabbage leaves, folding and tucking to enclose the layers completely.
5. Pour the broth into the pan, cover and bring to a boil. Reduce the heat to low and simmer for 35 minutes.
6. Remove the stuffed cabbage carefully, reserving the pan juices, and invert onto a serving platter.
7. Bring the pan juices to a boil in a small saucepan. Stir in the cornstarch mixture and cook until thickened, stirring constantly.
8. Pour the sauce over the stuffed cabbage, cut the cabbage into 6 portions and serve immediately.

YIELD: *6 servings.* **Nutritional Facts Per Serving:** Calories 210; Total Fat 13g (Saturated Fat 5g); Cholesterol 40mg; Sodium 570mg; Total Carbohydrate 11g (Dietary Fiber 3g; Sugars 5g); Protein 12g

Honey Apples (Northern Cuisine)

Ingredients:

2 medium apples
1 tablespoon all-purpose flour
2 tablespoons cornstarch

Batter:
3 tablespoons all-purpose flour
1 tablespoon cornstarch
1 tablespoon water
2 egg whites

Glazing Syrup:
2 tablespoons vegetable oil
1/4 cup maltose
1/4 cup honey

1 teaspoon vegetable oil
6 cups peanut or soybean oil for
    deep-frying
1 tablespoon white sesame seeds

Preparation:

- Peel and core the apples and cut each into 8 wedges.
- Place 1 tablespoon flour and 2 tablespoons cornstarch in a bag and shake to mix. Add the apples to the bag, shake until coated and set aside.
- Prepare the Batter by combining 3 tablespoons flour, 1 tablespoon cornstarch, 1 tablespoon water and the egg whites in a medium bowl and mix until the batter is smooth.
- Prepare the Glazing Syrup mixture by combining the 2 tablespoons vegetable oil, maltose and honey in a small bowl, blend well and set aside.
- Warm a serving plate, coat with about 1 teaspoon vegetable oil and set aside and keep warm.
- Prepare a bowl of ice water with about 8 ice cubes.

Procedure:

1. Heat the 6 cups peanut oil to 375 degrees in a deep fryer. Remove the apple wedges from the bag, dip the wedges in the Batter and place one at a time carefully in the hot oil; do not crowd. Deep-fry in three batches.
2. Deep-fry for about 3 minutes or until golden brown and drain on paper towels in a colander.
3. Preheat a wok. Add the Glazing Syrup mixture to the wok and bring to a boil, stirring constantly with cooking chopsticks. Cook to 275 degrees on a candy thermometer, soft-crack stage, or until the syrup forms long strings when dropped from a spoon.
4. Add the deep-fried apples all at once and stir quickly but gently until coated with the syrup. Sprinkle the sesame seeds on top and transfer to the heated serving plate.
5. Serve immediately with the bowl of ice water for serving as described in the sidebar at left.

As each piece of apple is picked up from the serving plate with chopsticks, the syrup is drawn into a glass-like thread, hence the alternative name for this recipe of drawn-thread apple. The apple piece, with the syrup threads, should be dipped quickly into ice water so that the syrup coating hardens instantly into a brittle candy coating with both taste and texture sensations.

YIELD: *6 servings.* **Nutritional Facts Per Serving:** Calories 270; Total Fat 15g (Saturated Fat 2g); Cholesterol 0mg; Sodium 20mg; Total Carbohydrate 34g (Dietary Fiber 1g; Sugars 20g); Protein 2g

Sesame Chicken in Yunnan Pot
(South-Western Cuisine) *(photo: page 73)*

Ingredients:

1 (2½-pound) frying chicken
2 dried black mushrooms
1 cup boiling water
1 green onion
¼ cup sesame oil
1 cup rice wine or pale dry sherry
1 tablespoon light soy sauce
1 teaspoon salt
1 teaspoon sugar
Dash of black or white pepper
2 slices fresh gingerroot

Preparation:

• Rinse the chicken with cold water and pat dry. Cut the chicken into 2½-inch pieces and set aside.
• Soak the mushrooms in 1 cup boiling water for 15 minutes. Drain the mushrooms, squeeze dry, cut off the stems and discard and slice the caps into halves.

• Cut the green onion into 2-inch pieces.
• Combine the sesame oil, rice wine, soy sauce, salt, sugar and pepper in a small bowl, mix well and set aside.

Procedure:

1. Layer the chicken pieces loosely in the Yunnan Pot. Pour the rice wine mixture over the chicken. Place the mushrooms, green onion pieces and gingerroot slices on top of the chicken.
2. Cover the Yunnan Pot and place the pot inside the Sandy Pot or on the top of a deep 3-quart saucepan about ⅓ filled with water.
3. Bring the water to a boil. Steam for about 45 minutes. The chicken will be very tender and the pan juices should be served over steamed rice.

YIELD: *8 servings.* **Nutritional Facts Per Serving:** Calories 320; Total Fat 27g (Saturated Fat 7g); Cholesterol 70mg; Sodium 440mg; Total Carbohydrate 2g (Dietary Fiber 0g; Sugars 1g); Protein 18g

A Yunnan Pot is a lidded earthenware casserole that has a center chimney rising from the bottom of the pot almost to the top. The Yunnan Pot is then placed in a larger pot, called the Sandy Pot and water added to the Sandy Pot. As the water in the Sandy Pot comes to a boil, the steam rises through the chimney to condense on the lid of the Yunnan Pot. This unique utensil and method of cooking is especially suitable for cooking at the high altitudes of the central-west province where Yunnan is located. Notice that water is not added directly to the chicken or meat. It is through the condensation of the water vapor that the chicken is cooked moist and tender, while rich delicious juice accumulates at the bottom. A good Dutch oven or casserole may be substituted for the authentic Yunnan Pot.

Cucumber Relish (Szechuan-Style)

Ingredients:

1¼ pounds cucumbers
1 tablespoon salt
2 garlic cloves, crushed
1 teaspoon Szechuan flower pepper
1 teaspoon hot bean paste
6 red chili peppers
1 teaspoon shredded fresh gingerroot
1 tablespoon chili sesame oil
1 tablespoon sugar
1 tablespoon rice vinegar
1 teaspoon dark soy sauce
¼ cup sesame oil

Preparation:

- Cut the ends from the cucumbers and discard. Cut each cucumber lengthwise into four strips about 2 inches long. Coat with salt and let stand for 1 hour.

- Combine the garlic, flower pepper, hot bean paste, chili peppers and gingerroot and set aside.
- Combine the chili sesame oil, sugar, rice vinegar and soy sauce in a small bowl and set aside.

Procedure:

1. Rinse the cucumbers with cold water, drain and pat dry and place in a large bowl.
2. Preheat a wok. Add the ¼ cup sesame oil and the garlic mixture and stir-fry for several seconds.
3. Add the soy sauce mixture and mix well. Pour the mixture over the cucumbers and mix gently to coat with the mixture.
4. Let the cucumbers stand for 3 hours or longer before serving. The cucumbers can be kept in a covered container in the refrigerator for up to one week.

YIELD: *6 servings.* **Nutritional Facts Per Serving:** Calories 110; Total Fat 9g (Saturated Fat 1.5g); Cholesterol 0mg; Sodium 480mg; Total Carbohydrate 7g (Dietary Fiber 1g; Sugars 4g); Protein 1g

Chinese Almond Cookies
(Traditional Dessert) *(photo: page 74)*

Ingredients:

8 ounces vegetable shortening
1/4 teaspoon yellow food coloring
2 1/2 cups all-purpose flour
1 1/4 cups sugar
1/2 teaspoon baking soda
1/2 teaspoon baking powder
1 egg
1/4 teaspoon sesame oil
2 teaspoons almond extract
1 cup blanched whole almonds

Preparation:

- Let the shortening stand at room temperature for one hour if it has been stored in the refrigerator.
- Combine the shortening and food coloring in a medium bowl and mix until the mixture is uniformly colored.
- Sift the flour, sugar, baking soda and baking powder together into a large bowl.
- Beat the egg in a small bowl. Add the sesame oil and almond extract, blend well and set aside.
- Crush half the almonds and set aside. Cut each remaining almond lengthwise into halves and set aside.

Procedure:

1. Preheat the oven to 375 degrees.
2. Add the colored shortening to the flour mixture and cut in until very fine crumbs form and the mixture resembles cornmeal.
3. Add the egg mixture and the crushed almonds and mix with fingers until the mixture holds together.
4. Shape the dough into 1-inch balls and arrange about 1 inch apart on an ungreased cookie sheet. Flatten the balls with the palm of the hand. Press an almond half onto each cookie.
5. Bake at 375 degrees for 10 minutes or until light golden brown. Let cool on the cookie sheet for about 1 minute and remove to a wire rack to cool completely.

YIELD: *12 (3-cookie) servings.* **Nutritional Facts Per Serving:** Calories 400; Total Fat 24g (Saturated Fat 4g); Cholesterol 20mg; Sodium 75mg; Total Carbohydrate 42g (Dietary Fiber 1g; Sugars 21g); Protein 5g

Chinese Fresh Noodles

Ingredients:

2 eggs
2 cups all-purpose flour
Pinch of salt
2 tablespoons cold water
Cornstarch

Procedure:

1. Beat the eggs in a medium bowl using cooking chopsticks.

2. Add the flour, salt and water and mix with the chopsticks until the mixture is crumbly and resembles cornmeal.

3. Continue mixing with moistened fingertips until the mixture holds together to form a dough.

4. Shape the dough into a ball and place in a clean bowl. Cover with a warm moist cloth and let stand for 30 minutes.

5. Divide the dough into 4 portions. Keep the unused portions covered with the moist cloth to prevent drying.

6. To shape the noodles using a manual (crank-style) pasta machine:

• Set the machine for #5 or the setting that will produce a smooth sheet of the dough. Feed one portion of the dough through the machine and sprinkle the sheet lightly with cornstarch.

• Set the machine for the desired thinness of the finished noodles and feed the dough sheet through the narrowest strip cutting slot.

• Repeat with the remaining dough portions.

7. To shape the noodles using an automatic pasta machine:

• Set the machine to the thickness that will result in the very thin noodles that are similar to angel hair pasta.

8. Use the noodles as desired. If the noodles will not be used immediately, dust lightly with cornstarch to prevent sticking and store in airtight plastic bags in the refrigerator.

YIELD: *6 servings.* **Nutritional Facts Per Serving:** Calories 180; Total Fat 2g (Saturated Fat 0.5g); Cholesterol 70mg; Sodium 20mg; Total Carbohydrate 32g (Dietary Fiber 0g; Sugars 0g); Protein 6g

Northern Cha-Chian Mein (Deep-Fried Bean Sauce Noodles) *(photo: page 74)*

Ingredients:

1 pound Chinese Fresh Noodles
  (page 98)
1 tablespoon sesame oil
1 tablespoon dried shrimp
2 large or 3 small dried black
  mushrooms
8 ounces lean pork
1 teaspoon cornstarch
1 tablespoon rice wine
4 ounces Chinese cabbage leaves
1 green onion
2 slices fresh gingerroot
1 garlic clove

Sauce:

$1/4$ cup bean sauce
1 tablespoon rice wine or pale dry sherry
2 tablespoons dark soy sauce
1 teaspoon chili sesame oil
$1/2$ teaspoon sugar

4 tablespoons vegetable oil
Dash of salt
$1/2$ cup chicken stock
$1/3$ cup cucumber
$1/3$ cup carrot

Preparation:

- Bring a generous amount of water
  to a boil in a large saucepan. Add the
  noodles. Cook for 3 minutes, stirring
  constantly with cooking chopsticks;
  drain well. Add the sesame oil, lifting
  with the chopsticks to coat lightly.
- Soak the dried shrimp and black
  mushrooms in boiling water to cover
  for 15 minutes. Trim off and discard
  the stems from the mushrooms and
  cut the caps into thin shreds.
- Dice the shrimp very small. Set the
  mushrooms and shrimp aside.

- Cut the pork into $1/4 \times 1/3 \times 1^1/2$-inch
  pieces and place in a bowl. Add 1
  teaspoon cornstarch and 1 tablespoon
  rice wine, mix well and set aside.
- Cut the cabbage leaves lengthwise
  into halves and then diagonally into
  $1/3 \times 1^1/2$-inch shreds and set aside.
- Cut the white of the green onion into
  $1/4$-inch dice and the green top into
  $1/4 \times 1$-inch diagonal shreds. Mince the
  gingerroot and garlic and set aside.
- Prepare the Sauce mixture by
  combining the bean sauce, rice wine,
  soy sauce, chili sesame oil and sugar
  in a small dish, mix well and set aside.
- Cut the cucumber and carrot into
  $1/4 \times 1/4 \times 1^1/2$-inch shreds.

Procedure:

1. Preheat a wok. Add 2 tablespoons of
   the oil. Add the pork and a dash of salt
   and stir-fry until the pork loses its
   pink color. Add the shrimp, mushrooms
   and cabbage and stir-fry for several
   seconds. Stir in the chicken stock and
   remove the pork mixture from the wok.
2. Heat the remaining 2 tablespoons oil
   in the wok. Add the white of the green
   onion, gingerroot and garlic and stir-
   fry until fragrant. Add the Sauce
   mixture and mix well.
3. Stir the pork mixture and the green
   onion top into the wok just until mixed.
4. Spread the noodles on the serving
   platter. Top the left $1/3$ of the noodles
   with the pork mixture, the right
   $1/3$ with the carrot shreds and the
   center $1/3$ with cucumber shreds.
5. Mix the noodles with the pork, carrots
   and cucumber in front of the diners.

YIELD: *6 servings.* **Nutritional Facts Per Serving:** Calories 350; Total Fat 14g (Saturated Fat 2g);
Cholesterol 95mg; Sodium 650mg; Total Carbohydrate 37g (Dietary Fiber 1g; Sugars 1g); Protein 17g

Dragon Phoenix Paradise
(Taiwanese Cuisine) *(photo: page 74)*

In Chinese cuisine, the recipe is named according to its value. This gourmet dish bears a fancy, mystical, romantic, and imaginative name. Dragon Phoenix symbolizes "Double Happiness." The colorful assortment of meats, pineapple chunks, and vegetables represents a look of paradise arrayed on a nest of puffed up bean threads resembling dragon fins. Traditionally, it is served in a New Year's banquet or other happy gathering.

Ingredients:
12 ounces boneless skinless
    chicken breast

Marinade:
1 egg white
1 tablespoon cornstarch
1 tablespoon light soy sauce
1 tablespoon rice wine or pale dry
    sherry

3 dried black mushrooms or
    6 straw mushrooms
4 ounces cooked ham
4 ounces Chinese cabbage
$1/3$ carrot
3 ears baby corn
3 water chestnuts
10 snow peas or 2 tablespoons shelled
    green peas
Whites of 2 green onions

Sauce:
$1 1/2$ cups chicken stock
1 tablespoon rice wine or pale
    dry sherry
1 teaspoon light soy sauce
$1/2$ teaspoon sugar
Dash of white or black pepper

1 tablespoon cornstarch
1 tablespoon water
6 cups peanut, corn, soybean or
    vegetable oil
2 ounces bean threads
2 tablespoons peanut, corn, soybean or
    vegetable oil
1 garlic clove, minced
2 slices fresh gingerroot, minced
$1/2$ teaspoon salt
$1/4$ cup sliced canned bamboo shoots
$1/4$ cup drained pineapple chunks
1 teaspoon sesame oil or chili oil

Preparation:
- Cut the chicken into $1/8 \times 1/2 \times 1$-inch slices and place in a bowl.
- Prepare the Marinade by beating the egg white in a small dish, add 1 tablespoon cornstarch, 1 tablespoon light soy sauce and 1 tablespoon rice wine and mix well.
- Pour the Marinade over the chicken and mix well to coat. Marinate the chicken in the refrigerator while preparing the vegetables.
- Soak the black mushrooms in boiling water to cover for 15 minutes. Drain and squeeze dry, trim and discard the stems, cut the caps into thirds and set aside.
- Cut the ham into pieces the same size as the chicken and set aside.
- Rinse the cabbage, pat dry, cut into $1/2 \times 2$-inch diagonal shreds and set aside.
- Peel the carrot, cut into 6 thin slices and then cut each slice into a flower shape and set aside.
- Cut the baby corn ears into halves and set aside
- Cut the water chestnuts into thin slices lengthwise and set aside.
- Snap both ends of the snow peas and set aside.
- Cut the green onions into $1/4$-inch dice.
- Prepare the Sauce mixture by combining the chicken stock, 1 tablespoon rice wine, 1 teaspoon light soy sauce, sugar and pepper in a small bowl, mix well and set aside.
- Dissolve 1 tablespoon cornstarch in 1 tablespoon water and set aside.

Procedure:

1. Heat the 6 cups peanut oil in a tempura pan, wok or deep-fryer to 350 to 375 degrees. Add the chicken pieces to the hot oil; do not crowd. Deep-fry for several seconds until light golden brown, remove with mesh-wire strainer to a plate.

2. Heat the oil until it is very hot, almost smoking, and add the bean threads. The bean threads will puff in seconds. Remove the bean threads to a preheated serving platter using a mesh-wire strainer. Arrange the bean threads on the platter to form a nest. Remove the hot oil from the heat and set aside for another use.

3. Heat 2 tablespoons peanut oil in a wok. Add the green onions, garlic and gingerroot and salt and stir-fry until light brown. Add the chicken, mushrooms, ham, Chinese cabbage, carrot slices, corn, water chestnuts, snow peas and bamboo shoots and stir-fry for several seconds.

4. Add the Sauce mixture and mix well. Cover the wok and bring the mixture to a boil.

5. Stir in the cornstarch and water mixture and cook until thickened, stirring constantly.

6. Add the pineapple chunks, sprinkle with the sesame oil and stir just once to mix.

7. Dish the hot mixture onto the nest of puffed bean threads quickly to make a sizzling sound and serve immediately.

YIELD: *6 servings.* **Nutritional Facts Per Serving:** Calories 260; Total Fat 15g (Saturated Fat 2.5g); Cholesterol 45mg; Sodium 810mg; Total Carbohydrate 11g (Dietary Fiber 1g; Sugars 2g); Protein 20g

Japanese Sushi

Japan is a nation of islands surrounded by water with an abundant supply of fresh seafood. Seafood makes up the main diet of the Japanese people, and, with rice and seaweed comprise the major ingredients of sushi. The origin of sushi comes of the practice of preserving fish by packing the fish between layers of rice that have had an acid-natured preservative, vinegar, added.

Japanese food is light, low in cholesterol, and nutritional. The rice has only 100 calories per 100 grams. The artistic presentation of sushi is as important as the taste of the fresh ingredients. Simplicity and elegance are the aesthetic factors that make sushi authentically Japanese.

The two most popular kinds of Sushi are: Maki-Zushi or Rolled Sushi shaped by rolling up with the use of a matchstick bamboo mat called "sudare." (Also see Nori-Maki Sushi in the Vegetarian section on page 156.) Nigiri-Zushi is hand-shaped, bite-size sushi. Both kinds of Sushi require a variety of rice that is different from the rice that is to be served as steamed or fried rice. Prepare the rice precisely as described below.

Sushi Rice

I was born and raised eating both Japanese and Chinese food. Until the end of the Second World War, Taiwan had been under Japanese rule for fifty years. I attended a Japanese elementary school. We carried our lunches, Sushi, in lunch cases called "bento." Sushi means "vinegared rice."

Ingredients:
2 cups Japan Calrose or Kokuho round
    grain rice
2$^1\!/_2$ cups water
1 (2 × 4-inch) piece Konbu
    (dried kelp)
$^1\!/_4$ cup rice vinegar
2 tablespoons sugar
$^1\!/_4$ teaspoon salt
1 cup water
2 tablespoons rice vinegar

Preparation:
- Combine the rice and the 2$^1\!/_2$ cups water in a saucepan.
- Add the Konbu. Bring the mixture to a boil, remove the Konbu and discard, cover the saucepan, reduce the heat to very low or warm setting for 10 minutes.
- Turn the heat off, remove the cover, place a clean cloth over the saucepan and replace the cover. Let stand for 10 minutes.
- Combine the $^1\!/_4$ cup rice vinegar, sugar and salt, mix well and add to the rice, mixing well.
- Prepare the Tezu by mixing the 1 cup water with the remaining 2 tablespoons rice vinegar. (Tezu prevents the rice from sticking to fingers and utensils while preparing Sushi.)
- Coat a large wooden bowl or platter with Tezu and spread the rice in the prepared bowl. Fan the rice and toss lightly with chopsticks for about 10 minutes to cool the rice quickly and bring a pearl-like luster to the rice grains.

YIELD: *6 cups.* **Nutritional Facts Per Serving:** Calories 240; Total Fat 0g (Saturated Fat 0g); Cholesterol 0mg; Sodium 0mg; Total Carbohydrate 52g (Dietary Fiber 1g; Sugars 0g); Protein 4g

Maki-Zushi *(photo: page 74)*

Ingredients:

1 recipe Sushi Rice (page 102)
3 shiitake mushrooms (Japanese dried black forest mushrooms)
$3/4$ ounce Kanpyo (dried gourd shavings)
$1^1/2$ cups water
$1/4$ cup sugar
$1/3$ cup soy sauce
1 tablespoon rice wine
2 eggs
2 teaspoons sugar
Pinch of salt
1 teaspoon cornstarch
2 tablespoons vegetable oil
4 sheets Nori (dried seaweed)
$1/2$ cup Oboro (commercially cooked, mashed and sweetened codfish or shrimp powder)

Preparation:

- Prepare the Sushi Rice and set aside.
- Soak the mushrooms in boiling water to cover for 10 minutes, drain, squeeze dry, cut into shreds and set aside.
- Soak the Kanpyo in salted water to cover for 30 minutes and rinse. Place in a small saucepan, add water to cover and boil until soft. Drain and add the $1^1/2$ cups water, $1/4$ cup sugar, soy sauce, rice wine and the mushrooms. Cook until the liquid evaporates and the mixture is almost dry and set aside.
- Beat the eggs in a small bowl. Add the 2 teaspoons sugar, salt and cornstarch and mix well.
- Heat a small amount of the vegetable oil in a skillet or wok. Add a portion of the egg mixture and swirl the pan to spread the egg mixture into a thin sheet. Cook for several seconds until firm, turn the sheet over and remove to a cutting surface. Repeat with the remaining oil and egg mixture. Cut the egg sheets into $1/4$-inch strips and set aside.

Procedure:

1. Place a sheet of Nori on a bamboo mat. Spread $1^1/2$ cups of the Sushi Rice evenly over $2/3$ of the Nori, leaving far edge of the Nori uncovered. Be sure to dip your fingers in Tezu (see page 102) frequently to prevent sticking.

2. Arrange rows of Kanpyo and mushroom mixture, egg strips and Oboro across the Nori. Roll up the Nori as for a jelly roll, using the bamboo mat to roll and press together. Moisten the uncovered edge of the Nori with Tezu, finish rolling tightly and remove the bamboo mat.

3. Press the ends of the roll lightly to straighten and cut the roll into 8 pieces. Repeat with the remaining ingredients.

YIELD: 6 servings. **Nutritional Facts Per Serving:** Calories 280; Total Fat 2g (Saturated Fat 0.5g); Cholesterol 70mg; Sodium 25mg; Total Carbohydrate 56g (Dietary Fiber 1g; Sugars 0g); Protein 7g

Nigiri-Zushi

Ingredients:

> 1 recipe Sushi Rice
> Fresh ocean fish such as tuna, red
>   snapper, yellow tail, flounder, sea
>   bass, salmon or halibut
> 1 tablespoon green Wasabi
> 1½ teaspoons water
> Tezu (see page 102)

Preparation:

* Prepare the Sushi Rice and set aside.
* Cut the selected fish into thin squares
  about the width of four fingers
  (1 × 3-inches).
* Blend the green Wasabi with the water
  and set aside.
* Prepare the Tezu and set aside.

Procedure:

1. Shape the Sushi Rice into ping-pong
   size balls, using about 2 tablespoons of
   the rice for each. (Be sure to moisten
   the spoon and your fingers with
   the Tezu.)
2. If you are right handed, hold your left
   hand with the palm up. Place a slice
   of the fish across the four fingers of
   your hand. Place a dab of the Wasabi
   mixture in the center of the fish and
   place a rice ball on the Wasabi. Press
   the fish around the rice ball, using
   the fleshy part of your left palm
3. Turn the packet over and use the
   thumb and index finger of your right
   hand to press the fish firmly around
   the rice ball, turning clockwise once.
   Place on a serving plate and continue
   with the remaining fish and rice until
   all the ingredients are used.
4. Serve with Sweet Pickled Ginger
   (Amazu Shoga).

YIELD: *6 servings*. **Nutritional Facts Per Serving:** Calories 240; Total Fat 0g (Saturated Fat 0g); Cholesterol 0mg; Sodium 0mg; Total Carbohydrate 52g (Dietary Fiber 1g; Sugars 0g); Protein 4g

Sweet Pickled Ginger (Amazu Shoga) is a "must" to serve with Nigiri-Zushi. It is as essential as serving hot dogs with mustard.

Sweet Pickled Ginger (Amazu Shoga)

Ingredients:

> 1 large fresh young gingerroot
> 2 teaspoons salt
> 3 tablespoons sugar
> 6 tablespoons water
> ¾ cup rice vinegar

Preparation:

* Select young gingerroot that has a soft
  skin and is pale yellow in color. Peel
  the gingerroot and cut into paper-thin
  slices. Sprinkle with the salt and let
  stand overnight.
* Rinse the gingerroot slices with water
  and pat dry.

Procedure:

1. Place the gingerroot slices in a small
   saucepan and add water to cover.
   Bring to a boil.
2. Combine the sugar, 6 tablespoons
   water and rice vinegar in a 1-quart
   saucepan and bring to a boil at the
   same time as the gingerroot.
3. Drain the gingerroot and add to
   the sugar mixture. Cook until the
   gingerroot becomes a pinkish orange
   color. Remove from the heat, cool and
   store in a covered jar in the refrigerator.
   It will keep for several weeks.

Mongolian Hot Pot (or Fire Pot)

The modern version of the Fire Pot is electric and has a 3-stage switch: off, Low (400 watts) and High (800 watts) and has a capacity that will serve four or five. Always prepare the clear soup stock in advance, fill the pot two-thirds full with the stock, cover and turn on High. When the stock boils, add the harder vegetables, then add the meats, the softer vegetables and the noodles last. Vary the meats to your own tastes.

Ingredients:

- 1 package Nanka noodles
- 1 tablespoon sesame or vegetable oil
- 1 pound boneless skinless chicken breasts
- 8 ounces top round or flank steak
- 3 fresh bean cakes or 1 can bean curd
- 8 ounces snow peas
- 8 dried Chinese mushrooms or 4 ounces fresh mushrooms
- 2 carrots
- 8 fresh water chestnuts or 1 small can, drained
- 8 ounces Chinese cabbage
- 1 small can whole bamboo shoots, drained
- 1 cucumber
- 1 medium onion
- 3 scallions
- 1/4 cup soy sauce
- 2 tablespoons rice vinegar
- 6 cups soup stock
- Salt, pepper and sugar to taste
- 2 teaspoons sesame oil
- 1 tablespoon rice wine
- 1 small package bean threads (Saifun)

Preparation:

- Cook the noodles to boiling water in a pot for 3 minutes, stirring constantly. Drain, place on a platter and drizzle with 1 tablespoon sesame oil, tossing to coat. Place the noodles on a platter.
- Keep the meats, bean cakes and individual vegetables on separate platters as prepared.
- Cut all the meats about 1/8 inch thick. Cut the bean cakes into large cubes and set aside. Cut all the vegetables about 1/8 inch thick.
- Mix the soy sauce and 2 tablespoons rice vinegar in a small dish to serve with the cooked meats, vegetables and noodles as a dipping sauce.

Procedure:

1. Place the soup with the salt, pepper, sugar, 2 teaspoons sesame oil and rice wine in the cooking pot and bring to a boil on High.
2. Add layers of the ingredients in the following order: harder vegetables, meats, softer vegetables, bean threads and the cooked noodles. Cover and bring to a boil.
3. When the soup stock comes to the second boil, reduce the heat to Low, remove the meats and vegetables with a mesh scooper and serve immediately with the dipping sauce.
4. Bring the remaining soup stock to a boil on High and refill the pot with additional ingredients as desired. When all the meats and vegetables have been cooked, add any remaining cooked noodles to soak up the rich broth.

A large vessel with a central chimney into which glowing charcoal is placed to provide the heat to cook the ingredients is called a Fire Pot. The utensil, as well as the dish it prepares, began in Northern China, where the winters are bitterly cold. The dish is usually served at a banquet or large family gathering. The pot is placed in the center of a large round table symbolizing unity. The thermal efficiency of the vertical heating is far better that that of a traditional cooking pot which has the heat applied to the bottom. This technique prepares a highly nutritious and very digestible meal for all ages.

YIELD: *10 servings.* **Nutritional Facts Per Serving:** Calories 400; Total Fat 13g (Saturated Fat 2.5g); Cholesterol 80mg; Sodium 410mg; Total Carbohydrate 35g (Dietary Fiber 5g; Sugars 4g); Protein 38g

Peking Duck

Ingredients:

1 (5-pound) fat duck
2 scallions
2 slices fresh gingerroot
3 tablespoons honey, molasses, or
  corn syrup
2 tablespoons rice wine or pale
  dry sherry
1/8 teaspoon red food coloring
3 tablespoons Hoisin sauce
1 teaspoon soy sauce
1 teaspoon sesame oil
1 teaspoon sugar
20 (3-inch) scallion brushes (page 46)
20 Mandarin Thin Pancakes (page 46)

Preparation:

- Rinse the duck inside and out and pat dry. Tie the duck with a cord around the neck or looped under the wings to facilitate manipulating it in water. (If the neck has not been removed, pump air between the skin and the flesh at the neck opening to stretch the skin as much as possible.

- Bring enough water to a boil in a large pan to completely submerge the duck. Place the duck in the boiling water for 5 minutes. (Cut off the wing tips and reserve with the giblets to be added to the duck carcass for soup stock later.) Dry the duck inside and outside and place on a large platter.

- Cut the scallions into 2-inch lengths and combine with the gingerroot slices. Combine the honey, rice wine and food coloring in a bowl and add the scallions and gingerroot. Pour the mixture over the duck and rub the mixture inside and outside for 1 minute.

- Bend a piece of heavy wire to make a hook at each end. Insert one of the hooks through the tail end of the duck securely. Use a chopstick to spread the wings of the duck apart and secure the other end of the wire so that the duck is suspended over the platter to catch the drippings.

- Place the duck in cool airy place for 6 hours or longer or place in the air stream of an electric fan for 4 hours or longer.

- Combine the Hoisin sauce, soy sauce, sesame oil and sugar in a small dipping dish and mix well.

- Prepare the scallion brushes and place in ice water to curl.

Peking Duck is the noble celebrated banquet dish of Northern China. It is always served with Mandarin Thin Pancakes. The Thin Pancakes are also served with Moo Shi Pork (page 47).

Procedure:

1. Preheat the oven to 375 degrees. Place the duck breast side up on a rack in a roasting pan and roast for 1 hour.
2. Reduce the oven temperature to 300 degrees. Turn the duck breast side down on the rack and roast for 30 minutes.
3. Increase the oven temperature to 375 degrees. Turn the duck breast side up and roast for 30 minutes longer.
4. Place the duck on a cutting board. Cut the skin from the breast, sides and back into 2 × 3-inch rectangles and arrange in a single layer on a serving platter.
5. Cut the duck meat into 2¹/₂-inch pieces and arrange on a second platter.

Presentation:

- Arrange the platters of duck skin and meat, the Hoisin sauce mixture, the scallion brushes and the Mandarin Thin Pancakes conveniently.
- Use a scallion brush to brush a small amount of the sauce on a Pancake, add a piece of duck meat and a piece of the duck skin and the scallion brush, fold the Pancake over to enclose the filling and roll into a cylinder. Serve immediately.

YIELD: *10 servings.* **Nutritional Facts Per Serving:** Calories 260; Total Fat 20g (Saturated Fat 7g); Cholesterol 55mg; Sodium 70mg; Total Carbohydrate 7g (Dietary Fiber 0g; Sugars 6g); Protein 13g

Szechuan Cuisine

Famous Szechuan Dishes

INTRODUCTION: Special Ingredients / Flavors and Methods

Szechuan Cuisine

Szechuan, literally Four Rivers, is a well-watered plateau province in the central Southwest region of China. Protected by the surrounding torturous mountains, the heart of the province, known as the Red Basin in the upper basin of the Yangtze River, is large, fertile, and populous.

The climate is most noted for very hot and humid summers. Therefore, Szechuan food is hot to the taste; often four or five kinds of pepper are used in one dish. I still remember the first time I ate at a famous Szechuan restaurant in Taiwan. The food was fiery! I asked my father, a physician, "Why do Szechuanese eat such hot food?" His answer was, "Those who live on high altitude and far inland feel very uncomfortable during the summer months, so their bodies need extra-hot and spicy food to help perspire and create appetite."

In recent years there are increasing numbers of Szechuan restaurants opening in the major cities of the United States. The popularity of Szechuan cuisine is obviously increasing among those who like hot and spicy food. Szechuan cuisine is unique. It uses more meat, less cornstarch for thickening than Cantonese cuisine, and does not have many noodle dishes. Steamed rice is served at each meal. These are features appealing to the diet-conscious Americans.

The use of dried vegetables is essential in Szechuan cooking. Each has its own unique, special, authentic flavor and texture, giving a characteristic, interesting taste when combined with the meat and peppers in a dish. Since farming is limited mostly to summer, vegetable crops are often sun-dried, or salted into pickles as preserves for the long winter's use.

Special Ingredients

Flower Pepper

Flower Pepper is also known as Szechuan Pepper, Fagara, or Anise Pepper of China. The reddish-brown peppercorn is a regional product of Szechuan Province and is used a great deal in the native cooking. Its hotness is relatively mild, but it is valued for its flowery fragrance. There are two kinds available: seeded and the whole pepper. The seeded one is much better for the aroma and flavor that come only from the petal-like husks.

Hot Bean Sauce

Hot Bean Sauce is the very hot, reddish-brown bean sauce essential for Szechuan cooking. It provides plenty of hotness and is a key flavoring. The canned and bottled products vary greatly in salt content. The native brand is the best. It can be kept refrigerated in a tightly lidded jar or plastic container almost indefinitely.

Szechuan Mustard

Szechuan Mustard is also known as Szechuan Pickle, or Szechuan Cabbage. The highly salted heart of mustard green is coated sparingly with ground red chili peppers and spices and is then preserved in cans. After opening, the mustard can be kept refrigerated in a covered jar indefinitely.

Chili Sauce

Chili Sauce is extremely hot. It is made of red chili peppers, sesame oil, and salt.

Chili Oil

Chili Oil is also known as Hot Oil. It is made of a red-colored chili pepper with sesame oil. Sprinkle a few drops into a dish before serving to perk up the Szechuan flavor. It keeps at room temperature.

Orange Peel

Orange Peel, when dried, become brown chips that give unique, citrus sweet flavor to meats. Soak the dried orange peel in hot water before use. If unavailable, fresh tangerine peel can be sun-dried until hardened completely and used in the same manner.

Sesame Paste

Sesame Paste is a thick paste made from mashed sesame seeds and soybean oil. It is an excellent coating for flavoring cold dishes like meats or noodles.

Wood Ear

Wood Ear called Moo-Shi, is also known as Black Fungus. Cloud Ear is a finer, smaller, and more tender variety. It is related to the mushroom that grows on the bark of trees.

When purchased, it is a grayish black, ear-shaped dried fungus. After soaking in boiling water for 15 minutes, it will expand in size and soften, and is ready for slicing. It is a very popular ingredient in Szechuan cooking.

Bamboo Shoots

Bamboo Shoots are also called Winter Shoots in Chinese. The shoots of bamboo plants are more tender when picked in winter or early spring. Use the shoots as a complementary ingredient because of the light and crispy texture. Bamboo grows abundantly in Szechuan Province.

Bean Cake or Bean Curd

Bean Cake or Bean Curd is called dou-fu in Chinese or tofu in Japanese. It is made from an extract of soybeans. Highly nutritious, Chinese vegetarians use it as a meat substitute as it is very rich in protein. Bean cake is widely used in Szechuan dishes.

Vinegar

Vinegar made from rice is best for this cuisine, but only when genuinely brewed from rice. It tastes smoother and less sharp than western wine or cider vinegar.

In Szechuan cooking, vinegar is almost always used as an ingredient. It helps digest food in the body and creates appetite.

Flavors and Methods

Chengtu is a large city in Szechuan Province and the center of an exceptionally fertile region. Its cooking represents the main line of Szechuan Cuisine.

There are *seven flavors:* hot, sour, sweet, sesame, bitter, salty, and fragrant. They are carefully incorporated in a dish by the following *eight methods of cooking:*

Con-Shao

Con-Shao means *cooked-dry.* In this method, the meat or vegetable is first stir-fried with ginger, garlic, hot bean sauce, and wine. Then add a little soup stock and salt and continue cooking until the soup is almost evaporated. Lastly add sugar, vinegar, tomato ketchup, green onion garnish, and thicken the dish with cornstarch paste.

There are two degrees of hotness with the cooked-dry method: the hot one is applied to fish dishes and the mild to vegetable or shark's fin dishes.

Yu-Xiang

Yu-Xiang means *fish fragrance.* This method is very popular in Szechuan cooking. The fish-like aroma is produced by stir-frying the combination of garlic, ginger, green onion, and flower pepper in the oil. Since fish is scarce in this region, the people here enjoy making the dish with fish-like fragrance.

Yu-Xiang dishes have a reddish-brown color because chili sauce, red chili, hot bean sauce, sugar, vinegar, wine, and cornstarch are added.

Ma-La

Ma-La means *sesame hot.* The dishes cooked by this method are very peppery hot because of the mixture of chili sauce, chili oil (sesame oil with chili), and Szechuan flower pepper added along with soy sauce, sugar, salt, green onion, and ginger.

Suan-La

Suan-La means *hot and sour*. Hot refers to Szechuan flower pepper and chili oil. Sour is from vinegar. The combination of peppers and vinegar is excellent for hot and humid days. This dish has a deep golden brown color like Hot and Sour Soup (page 54). The rest of the ingredients are soy sauce, salt, wine, and a little sugar.

Con-Chao

Con-Chao means *dry-fried*. The method uses only a very little oil to stir-fry. The ingredients needed are chili pepper, flower pepper, hot bean sauce, sugar, wine, salt, garlic, green onion. No water or soup stock is used. The dish has a dark brown color, and the food is crisp.

Guai-Wei

Guai-Wei literally means *strange taste*. This and the next two methods refer to the sauce that is mixed and poured over the dish. Since there is no apparent taste to the sauce, the dish is called strange taste, which is composed of all five flavors: sweet, sour, hot, salty, and sesame.

Chiao-Ma

Chiao-Ma is pepper and sesame sauce mixed with crushed flower peppers, salt, sesame oil, soy sauce, vinegar, sugar, minced ginger, and finely diced green onion.

Hong-You

Hong-You means *red oil*. Red is the color of chili oil. This is an excellent sauce for pouring over the dish before serving.

Shredded Beef with Yu-Xiang Sauce *(photo: page 75)*

Yu-Xiang means fish aroma in Chinese. Because fish are scarce in Szechuan Province, the natives have looked for flavors that resemble fish. Years of experimenting developed a formula of garlic, ginger, green onions and peppers in very hot oil that produces the fish smell that in turn flavors the meat.

Ingredients:

12 ounces top round or flank steak

Marinade:
1 egg white
1 tablespoon cornstarch
1/2 teaspoon salt

2 tablespoons dried wood ear or 1/2 cup
  shredded fresh snow peas
1/2 cup bamboo shoots
1/4 cup carrot
2 green onions
1/2 teaspoon Szechuan flower pepper
4 dried or fresh red chili peppers
1 teaspoon hot bean sauce
1 teaspoon Hoisin sauce or sweet
  bean sauce

Yu-Xiang Sauce:
1 teaspoon sugar
1 teaspoon rice vinegar
1 tablespoon rice wine
1 1/2 teaspoons chili oil
4 1/2 teaspoons soy sauce
1 1/2 teaspoons cornstarch
1 tablespoon water

6 cups peanut or vegetable oil for
  deep-frying
2 tablespoons vegetable oil
2 garlic cloves, crushed, minced
2 slices fresh gingerroot, minced

Preparation:

- Cut the steak into 1/8 × 1/8 × 2-inch shreds and place in a bowl. Beat the egg white with 1 tablespoon cornstarch and 1/2 teaspoon salt, add to the steak and mix until coated. Set the steak aside to marinate for several minutes.

- Soak the wood ear in boiling water to cover for 15 minutes, drain and squeeze dry.
- Cut the wood ear, bamboo shoots, carrot and green onion tops into 1/8 × 1/8 × 2-inch shreds and set aside.
- Cut the whites of the green onions into 1/4-inch pieces and set aside.
- Crush the flower pepper with the wooden handle of the cleaver; trim the ends from the chili peppers, discard the seeds and set aside.
- Measure the hot bean sauce and Hoisin sauce and set aside.
- Prepare the Yu-Xiang Sauce by combining the sugar, vinegar, rice wine, chili oil, soy sauce, 1 1/2 teaspoons cornstarch and water in a small dish, blend well and set aside.

Procedure:

1. Heat the oil for deep-frying to 375 degrees. Add the steak strips and deep-fry until the strips change color, turning and separating with cooking chopsticks. Remove to drain on paper towels.

2. Heat 2 tablespoons oil in a wok over high heat. Add the garlic, gingerroot, flower pepper, chili peppers and whites of the green onions and stir-fry until fragrant.

3. Add the wood ear, bamboo shoots, carrot shreds, green onion tops, hot bean sauce and Hoisin sauce and stir-fry for several seconds just to mix.

4. Add the deep-fried steak strips and the Yu-Xiang Sauce and stir-fry to mix well. Serve immediately with steamed rice.

YIELD: *6 servings.* **Nutritional Facts Per Serving:** Calories 210; Total Fat 12g (Saturated Fat 2.5g); Cholesterol 30mg; Sodium 480mg; Total Carbohydrate 13g (Dietary Fiber 5g; Sugars 1g); Protein 16g

Hot and Spicy Fried Crabs with Sweet and Sour Sauce *(photo: page 75)*

Ingredients:

³/4 cup cornstarch
¹/4 teaspoon salt
2 dried red chili peppers
2 slices fresh gingerroot, minced
2 small garlic cloves, minced

Sweet and Sour Sauce:
¹/3 cup sugar
¹/3 cup rice vinegar
¹/3 cup water
2 tablespoons ketchup
¹/4 teaspoon salt
1 tablespoon sesame oil

1 teaspoon cornstarch
1 tablespoon water
6 small or 4 large live crabs
6 cups peanut or vegetable oil for
    deep-frying
2 tablespoons vegetable oil

Preparation:

- Combine ³/4 cup cornstarch and ¹/4 teaspoon salt and set aside.
- Cut the tips from the chili peppers, discard the seeds, cut into ¹/4-inch dice, combine with the gingerroot and garlic and set aside.
- Combine the sugar, rice vinegar, ¹/3 cup water, ketchup, ¹/4 teaspoon salt and sesame oil in a small bowl, mix well and set aside.
- Dissolve 1 teaspoon cornstarch in 1 tablespoon water and set aside.

Procedure:

1. Wear gloves while preparing the crabs. Place the live crabs in the sink and rinse with very hot running water until all movement stops. Open the head shells, cut off and discard the small legs. Crack the claws with a cracker or dull side of the cleaver for easier eating. Remove and discard the gills and cut the bodies into halves.

2. Heat the oil for deep-frying to 350 degrees. Roll the crabs in the cornstarch and salt mixture to coat well. Add the prepared crabs to the hot oil and deep-fry for 2 minutes. Remove with a mesh-wire strainer. Reheat the oil, add the crabs and deep-fry for 2 minutes longer. Remove to paper towels in a colander to drain.

3. Preheat a wok. Pour 2 tablespoons oil into the wok. Add the chili peppers, gingerroot and garlic and stir-fry until fragrant.

4. Add the crabs to the wok and stir-fry for several seconds. Add the Sweet and Sour Sauce mixture and stir-fry until the mixture is heated through.

5. Add the cornstarch dissolved in water and cook until thickened, stirring constantly. Serve immediately.

Although this dish is originally Cantonese, I have altered it with a tinge of Szechuan flavor.

YIELD: *5 servings.* **Nutritional Facts Per Serving:** Calories 220; Total Fat 14g (Saturated Fat 2g); Cholesterol 15mg; Sodium 350mg; Total Carbohydrate 20g (Dietary Fiber 0g; Sugars 14g); Protein 4g

Mongolian Lamb with Hot Sauce (photo: page 75)

This recipe originated in Shangtung Province and has been popular with Mongolians, the Chinese Moslems. The essence of making this dish superb is that the lamb should be sliced very thinly and cooked rapidly with leeks or green onions. The method of cooking is called Con-Chao, which means dry-fried. The first cooking is deep-fried, followed by the dry-fried step.

Chinese vegetarians prefer peanut oil for its fragrance and the good taste that it gives to a dish, as well as the characteristic of retaining high temperatures while smoking less than other vegetable oils.

Ingredients:

12 ounces boned leg of lamb, frozen

Marinade:
1 tablespoon rice wine or pale
   dry sherry
2 tablespoons dark soy sauce
1 tablespoon cornstarch
$1/2$ teaspoon salt
1 teaspoon sugar or honey

1 teaspoon vegetable oil
Whites of 2 leeks or 4 green onions
4 garlic cloves, minced
2 red chili peppers
$1/2$ teaspoon Szechuan flower pepper,
   crushed
$1/4$ cup bamboo shoots

Seasoning Sauce:
$1^1/2$ teaspoons hot bean sauce
$1^1/2$ teaspoons dark soy sauce
1 tablespoon rice vinegar
1 teaspoon sugar
1 teaspoon sesame oil

6 cups peanut or soybean oil for
   deep-frying
2 tablespoons vegetable oil
Green tops of 2 leeks, shredded

Preparation:

- Partially thaw the lamb. Cut the lamb into $1/8 \times 3/4 \times 1^1/2$-inch pieces.
- Mix 1 tablespoon rice wine, 2 tablespoons soy sauce, cornstarch, salt and 1 teaspoon sugar together in a small bowl. Pour the Marinade over the lamb and toss to coat. Drizzle 1 teaspoon oil over the top to prevent drying. Let stand to marinate for 15 minutes.
- Cut the leeks into $1/3 \times 1^1/2$-inch shreds, mix whites of leeks with the garlic and set aside.
- Trim the ends from the chili peppers, discard the seeds, combine with the flower pepper and set aside.
- Cut the bamboo shoots into the same size pieces as the lamb and set aside.
- Prepare the Seasoning Sauce by combining the hot bean sauce, $1^1/2$ teaspoons dark soy sauce, 1 tablespoon rice vinegar, 1 teaspoon sugar and sesame oil, mix well and set aside.

Procedure:

1. Preheat the oil for deep-frying to 375 degrees. Add the lamb and deep-fry for several seconds and remove to drain.
2. Preheat a wok. Add 2 tablespoons vegetable oil, the whites of leeks and garlic, and peppers. Stir-fry until fragrant.
3. Add the bamboo shoots, the Seasoning Sauce mixture, the lamb and the green leek shreds and stir-fry until well mixed. Serve immediately.

YIELD: *4 servings.* **Nutritional Facts Per Serving:** Calories 300; Total Fat 21g (Saturated Fat 4g); Cholesterol 55mg; Sodium 780mg; Total Carbohydrate 9g (Dietary Fiber 1g; Sugars 2g); Protein 19g

Ma-Po's Bean Curd

Ingredients:

1 pound fresh bean cake
2 green onions
2 slices fresh gingerroot
1 large or 2 small garlic cloves

Brown Sauce:
1 tablespoon soy sauce
1 tablespoon rice wine or pale
   dry sherry
1 cup water
1 teaspoon sugar
$1/2$ teaspoon salt

2 teaspoons cornstarch
2 teaspoons water
2 tablespoons vegetable oil
4 ounces ground pork
1 tablespoon hot bean sauce
1 teaspoon chili oil
$1/2$ teaspoon Szechuan flower pepper

Preparation:

- Cut the bean cake into $1/2$-inch cubes and place in a deep bowl. Cover the cubes with boiling water and let stand for several minutes until the bean cake cubes have hardened slightly. Drain well and set aside.
- Cut the whites of the green onions into $1/4$-inch dice and the green tops into $1/8$-inch dice. Set the white and green portions aside separately. Mince the gingerroot and garlic.

- Prepare the Brown Sauce by combining the soy sauce, rice wine, 1 cup water, sugar and salt in a small bowl, mix well and set aside.
- Dissolve 2 teaspoons cornstarch in 2 teaspoons water and set aside.

Procedure:

1. Preheat a wok. Add the vegetable oil, whites of the green onions, gingerroot and garlic and stir-fry until the green onion is light brown. Add the pork and hot bean sauce and stir-fry until the pork is no longer pink.
2. Add the Brown Sauce mixture and stir until mixed. Add the bean cake cubes gradually. Cover the wok and bring to a boil.
3. Add the cornstarch dissolved in water and cook until thickened, stirring carefully.
4. Drizzle with the chili oil and sprinkle with the flower pepper and green onion tops. Serve immediately with steamed rice.

YIELD: *5 servings.* **Nutritional Facts Per Serving:** Calories 180; Total Fat 12g (Saturated Fat 1.5g); Cholesterol 15mg; Sodium 580mg; Total Carbohydrate 6g (Dietary Fiber 1g; Sugars 1g); Protein 13g

This recipe takes its name from the wife of a restaurant owner, Chen Fu-Chih, in Chengtu City during the 1860s. It is also known as Chen Ma-Po's Dou-Fu. Dou-Fu means bean curd or bean cake; it is a protein substitute used by Chinese vegetarians. Vegetarians should be sure to use dried black mushrooms rather than the ground pork.

When substituting with mushrooms, soak 2 dried black mushrooms in boiling water for 15 minutes. When soft, cut into dices before using.

Cheng-Tu Chicken

Cheng-Tu is a large city located in Szechuan Province. The cooking of the province is the origin and center of Szechuan cuisine. Plain stir-fried spinach or snow peas is a very good accompaniment to this dish.

Ingredients:

1 pound boneless skinless chicken breasts

Marinade:
1 tablespoon light soy sauce
4^1/$_2$ teaspoons cornstarch
1 tablespoon rice wine or pale dry sherry
^{1}/$_4$ teaspoon salt

2 green onions
4 red chili peppers
2 thin slices fresh gingerroot, minced
3 large or 4 small garlic cloves, minced
1 tablespoon hot bean sauce

Szechuan Sauce:
1 tablespoon dark soy sauce
2 teaspoons sugar
1 teaspoon rice vinegar
1^1/$_2$ teaspoons rice wine or pale dry sherry
^{1}/$_2$ teaspoon crushed flower pepper
1 teaspoon chili oil
1 teaspoon cornstarch
1 teaspoon cold water

6 cups peanut oil or vegetable oil for deep-frying
2 tablespoons vegetable oil

Preparation:

- Cut the chicken into ^{1}/$_4$ × ^{3}/$_4$ × 1-inch pieces and place in a bowl. Combine the light soy sauce, 4^1/$_2$ teaspoons cornstarch, 1 tablespoon rice wine and salt in a small bowl. Mix well and pour over the chicken, mixing to coat. Marinate for 20 minutes.
- Cut the green onions into ^{1}/$_4$-inch pieces. Cut the tips from the chili peppers and discard the seeds. Combine the green onions, chili peppers, gingerroot, garlic and hot bean sauce and set aside.
- Prepare the Szechuan Sauce by combining 1 tablespoon dark soy sauce, sugar, rice vinegar, 1^1/$_2$ teaspoons rice wine, flower pepper, chili oil, 1 teaspoon cornstarch and 1 teaspoon water, mix well and set aside.

Procedure:

1. Heat the oil for deep-frying to 375 degrees. Add the chicken carefully to the hot oil, deep-fry until the chicken turns white and drain on paper towels in a colander.
2. Heat 2 tablespoons oil in a wok. Add the green onion mixture and stir-fry until fragrant.
3. Add the chicken to the wok and stir in the Szechuan Sauce mixture. Stir-fry just until heated through and serve immediately.

YIELD: *4 servings.* **Nutritional Facts Per Serving:** Calories 290; Total Fat 16g (Saturated Fat 2g); Cholesterol 65mg; Sodium 470mg; Total Carbohydrate 8g (Dietary Fiber 0g; Sugars 2g); Protein 27g

Twice-Cooked Pork *(photo: page 75)*

Ingredients:

1 pound pork
1 teaspoon salt
2 slices fresh gingerroot
1 green onion
3 dried wood ears
1 green bell pepper
8 ounces cabbage
2 green onions
4 small garlic cloves
1 1/2 teaspoons Hoisin sauce
1 1/2 teaspoons hot bean sauce
1 tablespoon rice wine or pale
    dry sherry
1 tablespoon dark soy sauce
1 teaspoon sugar
Dash of black or white pepper
1 teaspoon cornstarch
2 teaspoons water
4 tablespoons vegetable oil
1/2 teaspoon salt

Preparation:

- Place the pork in a deep saucepan. Add enough water to cover, 1 teaspoon salt, gingerroot and 1 green onion and bring to a boil. Reduce the heat and simmer, covered, for 20 minutes. Remove the pork and let stand until cool. Reserve the stock for soup at a later time. Cut the pork into 1-inch squares sliced 1/8 inch thick.
- Soak the wood ears in boiling water to cover for 15 minutes. Drain, cut into pieces the same size as the pork and set aside.

- Discard the seeds and membranes from the green pepper and cut into 1-inch squares. Cut the cabbage into 1-inch squares and set the cabbage and green pepper aside.
- Cut the white and green of the 2 green onions into 1/4-inch dice and set aside separately. Mince the garlic.
- Measure out separately the Hoisin sauce, hot bean sauce, rice wine, dark soy sauce, sugar and pepper and set aside.
- Dissolve the cornstarch in 2 teaspoons water and set aside.

Procedure:

1. Preheat a wok. Add 2 tablespoons of the oil and 1/2 teaspoon salt and swirl to coat the wok evenly. Add the green pepper and cabbage and stir-fry for several seconds. Remove the vegetables.
2. Reheat the wok and add the remaining 2 tablespoons oil. Add the diced white of the green onions and garlic and stir-fry until fragrant. Add the wood ears, Hoisin sauce, hot bean sauce and pork and stir-fry for several seconds. Add the vegetables, rice wine, dark soy sauce, sugar and pepper and mix well.
3. Stir in the cornstarch mixture and cook until thickened, stirring constantly. Garnish with the diced green of the green onions. Serve immediately.

In Chinese this dish is Huai-Kuo-Juo, which literally means "Returned to the Pot Pork." A whole piece of pork is first boiled, cooled, sliced and then stir-fried with the other ingredients. It is sometimes called Double-Cooked Pork.

YIELD: *6 servings.* **Nutritional Facts Per Serving:** Calories 220; Total Fat 13g (Saturated Fat 2g); Cholesterol 50mg; Sodium 720mg; Total Carbohydrate 7g (Dietary Fiber 1g; Sugars 3g); Protein 18g

Eggplant Szechuan-Style *(photo: page 76)*

In Chinese this dish is called Yu-Xiang Eggplant which means that it is cooked according to the popular Yu-Xiang method, meaning "fish-fragrance." The fish-like aroma melds with the pork flavors to make the eggplant an exciting specialty.

Ingredients:

1 pound eggplant
2 green onions
2 slices fresh gingerroot
4 garlic cloves
1/2 teaspoon flower pepper

Yu-Xiang Sauce:

1 tablespoon soy sauce
1 tablespoon rice wine
1 1/2 teaspoons rice vinegar
2 teaspoons sugar
1/2 teaspoon salt

1 teaspoon cornstarch
1 teaspoon water
6 cups peanut or vegetable oil for deep-frying
2 tablespoons peanut oil
4 ounces ground pork
1 1/2 teaspoons hot bean sauce
1/2 cup soup stock or water
1 teaspoon chili oil

Preparation:

- Trim the ends from the eggplant, peel and cut into 1/2 × 3/4 × 2-inch pieces and set aside.
- Cut the whites of the green onions into 1/4-inch dice, cut the green tops into 1/8-inch dice and set aside separately. Mince the gingerroot and garlic and crush the flower pepper with a mortar and pestle.
- Combine the Yu-Xiang Sauce ingredients in a small bowl, mix well and set aside.
- Dissolve the cornstarch in 1 teaspoon water.

Procedure:

1. Heat the oil for deep-frying to 375 degrees. Add the eggplant pieces and deep-fry until soft, remove with a strainer to a colander lined with paper towels and press to remove the excess oil.
2. Preheat a wok. Add 2 tablespoons peanut oil, whites of the green onions, gingerroot, garlic, and flower pepper and stir-fry until fragrant. Add the pork and hot bean sauce and stir-fry until the pork is cooked through.
3. Add the eggplant and Yu-Xiang Sauce mixture and stir-fry for several seconds. Add the soup stock and stir-fry until well mixed.
4. Bring the mixture to a boil. Stir in the cornstarch mixture and cook until thickened, stirring constantly. Sprinkle with the chili oil and the green onion tops and serve immediately.

YIELD: *5 servings.* **Nutritional Facts Per Serving:** Calories 210; Total Fat 17g (Saturated Fat 3g); Cholesterol 15mg; Sodium 550mg; Total Carbohydrate 10g (Dietary Fiber 2g; Sugars 5g); Protein 6g

Steamed Beef with Spicy Rice Crumb

If Szechuan spicy rice crumb is unobtainable, prepare your own by pan-frying ³/₄ cup uncooked glutinous rice with a mixture of 1 teaspoon crushed flower pepper and ¹/₂ teaspoon five-spice powder in a dry wok or skillet until light brown and then grinding the rice mixture finely with a mortar and pestle.

Ingredients:

- 1 pound top round or flank steak
- 2 tablespoons dark soy sauce
- 2 tablespoons vegetable oil
- 2 tablespoons rice wine or pale dry sherry
- 1 teaspoon hot bean sauce
- 3 slices fresh gingerroot, minced
- Whites of 2 green onions, diced
- 1 teaspoon sugar
- 3 tablespoons water
- ³/₄ cup (5 ounces) Szechuan rice crumb
- 1 teaspoon chili oil
- 1 teaspoon sesame oil
- Green tops of 2 green onions, diced

Preparation:

- Cut the beef into 1¹/₂-inch squares that are ¹/₈ inch thick. Combine the soy sauce, vegetable oil, rice wine, hot bean sauce, gingerroot, whites of green onions, sugar and water in a large bowl and mix well. Add the beef and stir with cooking chopsticks to mix well. Marinate for 15 minutes.
- Add the rice crumb to the beef and mix very well with fingers.
- Stretch moist, oiled cheesecloth over each of the stacking bamboo steamer racks. Arrange the coated beef pieces evenly on the cheesecloth.

Procedure:

1. Pour enough water into a wok to half-fill and bring the water to a boil. Place the bamboo steamer over the boiling water, making sure that the water does not reach the level of the bottom rack. Cover the steamer, maintain a vigorous boil and steam for 25 minutes.

2. Remove the beef to a heated serving dish, sprinkle with the chili and sesame oils and green onion tops and toss to mix. Serve immediately.

Take care of your bamboo steamer. Do not soak in either clear or soapy water to prevent warping. Prevent food sticking to the steamer by lining with cheesecloth that has been moistened with warm water, oiled, and stretched to cover the racks.

YIELD: *4 servings.* **Nutritional Facts Per Serving:** Calories 350; Total Fat 12g (Saturated Fat 2g); Cholesterol 65mg; Sodium 640mg; Total Carbohydrate 29g (Dietary Fiber 1g; Sugars 1g); Protein 29g

Soy-Bean Sauce Pork

This very popular appetizer of Mandarin and Szechuan Cuisine can be served at room temperature or cold. The all-around wonderful flavor comes from the dried orange peel, star anise, flower pepper and other seasonings that interact with the pork.

Ingredients:

1 pound center-cut pork loin
3 tablespoons Hoisin sauce or sweet bean sauce
2 tablespoons rice wine or pale dry sherry
3 cups water
1/2 cup soy sauce
1/2 teaspoon flower pepper, crushed
3 pieces star anise
4 small or 3 large pieces dried orange peel
2 garlic cloves, crushed
2 green onions, cut into 3-inch pieces
2 slices fresh gingerroot, minced

Preparation:

- Cut the pork into 3 strips that measure 1 × 2 × 6-inches and place in a shallow dish. Mix the Hoisin sauce and rice wine in a small bowl and pour over the pork, spreading evenly on all sides. Marinate in the refrigerator for 4 to 6 hours.

Procedure:

1. Bring the water to a boil in a saucepan or wok. Add the soy sauce, flower pepper, star anise, dried orange peel, garlic, green onions and gingerroot and mix well.
2. Add the marinated pork with the marinade to the saucepan, cover and reduce the heat to a simmer. Simmer for 1 hour or until tender, turning the pork occasionally.
3. Remove the pork from the saucepan and set aside to cool. Skim the cooking juices.

Presentation:

- Cut the cooled pork into thin slices and arrange on a serving platter. Garnish the plate with parsley, lettuce and tomato. Pour the skimmed cooking juices into a shallow dish for dipping and mix in a few drops of chili oil.

YIELD: *6 servings.* **Nutritional Facts Per Serving:** Calories 130; Total Fat 4g (Saturated Fat 1.5g); Cholesterol 50mg; Sodium 1080mg; Total Carbohydrate 6g (Dietary Fiber 0g; Sugars 3g); Protein 18g

Steamed Lotus Leaf Buns

Ingredients:

- 1 cup all-purpose flour
- $\frac{1}{2}$ cup cake flour
- 2 teaspoons baking powder
- $\frac{1}{4}$ cup vegetable shortening
- 1 tablespoon sugar
- $\frac{1}{3}$ cup cold water
- 2 tablespoons sesame oil

Preparation:

- Sift the flours and baking powder into a bowl. Add the shortening, sugar and water and mix with cooking chopsticks or a rubber spatula until a soft dough forms.

- Gather the mixture into a ball and knead on a lightly floured surface until the dough is smooth. Shape into a rope about 1-inch in diameter and 16 inches long. Cut into 16 equal portions.

- Shape the buns by flattening each portion with the palm of your hand on a lightly floured surface and then rolling into a 4-inch circle. Brush the top with an ample amount of the 2 tablespoons sesame oil and fold over to form a half-circle. (If enough sesame oil is not applied, the buns cannot be opened into a pouch, with the meat and vegetable slices put in between, and eaten like a sandwich.)

- Score the top diagonally in a grid pattern using the dull side of a cleaver or spatula. Make a small indentation in the outer edge of the half-circle about 1 inch from each corner. The final shape will resemble a closed lotus leaf.

Procedure:

1. Arrange the buns on oiled aluminum steamer racks or bamboo steamer racks lined with moistened, oiled cheesecloth, leaving about 1 inch between the buns.

2. Bring enough water to a boil in a wok to steam the buns. Do not allow the water to touch the racks. Place the steamer racks over the boiling water and steam for 8 minutes.

3. Serve immediately while hot, soft, and fluffy with Fragrant Crispy Duck (page 124), flower pepper salt (page 125) and Hoisin sauce. Garnish with tomato slices and lettuce.

YIELD: *6 servings.* **Nutritional Facts Per Serving:** Calories 230; Total Fat 13g (Saturated Fat 2.5g); Cholesterol 0mg; Sodium 120mg; Total Carbohydrate 25g (Dietary Fiber 0g; Sugars 2g); Protein 3g

Fragrant Crispy Duck (photo: page 76)

This Szechuan dish is as celebrated as Peking Duck is to Mandarin Cuisine. Giving the finished duck a very light, crispy skin and fragrant meat requires long and careful preparation. Soaking (marinating) and drying are essential to making this dish successful. Traditionally, Crispy Duck is served with flower pepper salt (see sidebar, page 125) and Lotus Leaf Buns (page 123).

Ingredients:

1 duck
1 tablespoon Szechuan flower pepper
4 star anise
5 slices fresh gingerroot, minced
3 green onions, finely diced
2 tablespoons salt
2 tablespoons rice wine
1 tablespoon sweet fennel (optional)
3 tablespoons soy sauce
1 tablespoon rice wine
¼ cup cornstarch
¼ cup water chestnut powder
6 to 8 cups peanut oil for deep-frying
Hoisin sauce or sweet bean sauce

Preparation:

- Clean and rinse the duck inside and outside. Pat the duck dry inside and out.
- Hang the duck by the tail in a cool place. Let dry for 2 hours or place in the air stream of an electric fan for 30 minutes.
- Crush the flower pepper and star anise with a mortar and pestle and mix with the gingerroot, green onions, salt, 2 tablespoons rice wine and fennel. Rub the mixture over the duck inside and out and marinate for 30 minutes.
- Blend the soy sauce and 1 tablespoon rice wine and set aside.
- Mix the cornstarch with the water chestnut powder and set aside.

Procedure:

1. Place the marinated duck in a steamer and steam for 1½ hours or until very tender. Remove the duck from the steamer and let stand until cool.
2. Cut the duck carefully into halves down the breast bone and along the back bone.
3. Rub the duck with the soy sauce mixture and roll in the cornstarch mixture to coat well.
4. Preheat the peanut oil to 400 degrees in a large deep fryer. Place the duck in the hot oil carefully and deep fry briefly. Reduce the heat to medium and deep-fry until golden brown. Remove the duck to paper towels to drain and cool slightly.
5. Cut the duck into bite-size pieces with a cleaver.

YIELD: *6 servings.* **Nutritional Facts Per Serving:** Calories 260; Total Fat 16g (Saturated Fat 4g); Cholesterol 85mg; Sodium 920mg; Total Carbohydrate 7g (Dietary Fiber 0g; Sugars 0g); Protein 21g

Presentation:

- Arrange the pieces of duck on a platter assembled to resemble the whole duck. Garnish the platter with thin slices of tomato and shreds of lettuce.
- Serve with Lotus Leaf Buns, flower pepper salt (see sidebar at right) and a dipping sauce of Hoisin sauce or sweet bean sauce.

Prepare the flower pepper salt by stir-frying 1 tablespoon salt and 1 tablespoon crushed flower pepper in a dry wok until the salt is light brown and fragrant. Set aside in a small dip dish to serve with the duck.

Hunan Cuisine

Famous Hunan Dishes

INTRODUCTION: Ingredients

Hunan Cuisine

H unan, literally meaning "Lake South or South of the Lake," is a province in South-Central China between Canton and Szechuan. It is located in the geographic zone of Two Lakes Basin, together with Hupei (Lake North) Province. The entire basin is filled with numerous lakes and rivers merging into the mighty Yangtze, thus Hunan is a well-watered, verdant province. Dong-Ting Lake in the Northeastern corner is rich in marine life and the center of Hunan's gastronomic wealth.

Unlike Szechuan Province, Hunan has a gentle topography suitable for farming. It is blessed with fertile soil, natural resources, abundant rainfall, and a warm climate. Hunan is China's agricultural heartland which produces a wide range of cultivated food including rice wheat, soybeans, fruits, vegetables, meat, fowl, and freshwater fish.

Hunan cuisine bears a strong resemblance to the fiery hot cooking of Szechuan. Both provinces are situated inland and surrounded by mountains which hinder the normal circulation of air, therefore causing long, hot, and humid summers. It has been found that by adding many chili peppers and spices to the food, perspiration can be induced which allows for easier breathing and relieves the heat and humidity.

Hunan food is hearty and varies from sweet and sour dishes to cured and smoked meat, fowl, and fish to the slow-cooked Hunan Pot with clear soup. The most famous smoked dish is Tea-Smoked Duck (page 40). Smoking is the process of adding flavor to meat rather than simply preserving. The duck is flavored by smoking over sugar, rice, tea leaves, and camphor wood chips.

Another popular method in Hunan is curing, marinating, or pickling the meat, fish, or poultry before cooking. This is a way to preserve it from spoiling in the hot and humid climate. An example is Dry Marinated Pork. Honey-Glazed Ham (page 136) is also a Hunan specialty dish.

Ingredients

Fermented Black Beans

Fermented Black Beans are one of the most important condiments in Hunan cooking. They are used as a salt replacement and as a key flavoring. Liu-Yang County in Hunan is noted for producing the best fermented black beans in China.

The complexity and fragrance of Hunan Sauce is as a result of many varied spices (such as garlic, ginger, green onion, chili peppers, dry mustard and fermented black beans) which stimulate the appetite.

Bean Curd and Wood Ear

Bean Curd and Wood Ear are often used in Hunan cuisine. Bean Curd or bean cake (called dou-fu in Chinese) is made from an extract of soybeans, and is a protein substitute for vegetarians.

Wood Ear or Tree Ear (called Moo-Shi in Chinese) is also known as Black Fungus. It is related to the mushroom and grows on the bark of a tree.

Cloud Ear

Cloud Ear is the small and tender variety of Wood Ear. Hunan produces the best black, and white, cloud ears which have an interesting texture. They are low in calories, yet high in nutritional value.

White Wood Ear, also called Silver Ear, is a pale cream-coloured lichen that looks crinkly after being sun-dried. It is more rare than black fungus, and also more expensive. Steamed with rock sugar, silver ear is considered to be a medicinal food.

Dried Black Mushrooms, Tiger Lily (or Golden Needle), Orange Peel, and Dried Shrimp

Dried Black Mushrooms (page 20), Tiger Lily, Orange Peel (page 110), and Dried Shrimp (page 20) are important complements, adding certain distinctive flavor, fragrance, and texture to the dish. Beef with Orange Peel (page 130) is a well-known Hunan dish.

Tiger Lily, also called Golden Needle, are buds from the tiger lily flower that are sun-dried. The color turns dark golden brown after drying, and the pointed tip is what gives it the name of needle. The Chinese believe that this herb has medicinal value.

Vinegar

Vinegar is an essential ingredient which helps to digest food in the body. The sour taste of vinegar is usually balanced with sugar and other spices, adding an intricate flavor to Hunan dishes.

Star Anise

Star Anise is an eight-angled star-shaped spice with a strong aniseed flavor. It is often used in cooking with meat to give a rich and strong flavored sauce.

Chili Peppers and Other Flavors

Chili Paste, Chili Oil, Hot Bean Sauce, Hot Black Bean Sauce, Sesame Oil, Sesame Seeds, Sesame Paste, and Flower Pepper are all used in both Hunan and Szechuan cooking.

Four or five kinds of chili peppers (fresh or dried) are used in one dish to make Hunan cooking the hottest in China. Steamed rice and hot tea are good to accompany this hot and spicy food.

Beef with Orange Peel

Ingredients:

1 pound lean top round or flank steak
1 tablespoon dark soy sauce
1 tablespoon rice wine or pale
   dry sherry
1 teaspoon baking soda
1 teaspoon sugar
Pinch of black or white pepper
1 teaspoon vegetable oil
6 (1-inch) rounds dried orange peel
4 to 6 red chili peppers
4 garlic cloves, minced
2 slices fresh gingerroot, minced
2 green onions

Orange Sauce:

$2/3$ cup fresh orange juice or reserved
   orange peel soaking liquid
3 tablespoons sugar
1 tablespoon rice vinegar
$1^1/2$ teaspoons soy sauce
1 teaspoon sesame chili oil
Small pinch of salt

1 teaspoon cornstarch
2 teaspoons water
1 egg, beaten
$1/3$ cup cornstarch
4 to 6 cups peanut oil for deep-frying
2 tablespoons vegetable oil

Preparation:

- Cut the steak into $1/4 \times 1 \times 2$-inch pieces and place in a bowl.
- Combine 1 tablespoon soy sauce, rice wine, baking soda, sugar and pepper, mix well and pour over the steak, tossing to coat. Drizzle 1 teaspoon oil over the top to prevent drying. Let the steak stand for 30 minutes to marinate.
- Soften the dried orange peel by soaking in boiling water to cover.

Drain, reserving the liquid if desired, chop the orange peel finely and set aside.
- Cut the ends from the chili peppers, tap to remove and discard the seeds and cut the pods into $1/4$-inch dice. Combine with the orange peel, garlic and gingerroot and set aside.
- Cut the green onions into $1/8$-inch dice and set the white and green portions aside separately.
- Combine the Orange Sauce ingredients in a small dish, mix well and set aside.
- Dissolve 1 teaspoon cornstarch in 2 teaspoons water and set aside.
- Add the egg to the steak mixture and mix well. Add the $1/3$ cup cornstarch and toss until the steak pieces are well coated.

Procedure:

1. Heat the 4 to 6 cups peanut oil to 375 degrees. Deep-fry several pieces of the steak at a time and drain on paper towels.
2. Heat a wok. Add the 2 tablespoons oil and swirl to coat the wok. Add the white of the green onions and chili pepper mixture and stir-fry until fragrant.
3. Add the Orange Sauce to the wok and cook until the mixture comes to a boil, stirring constantly.
4. Add the cornstarch dissolved in water and cook until thickened, stirring constantly.
5. Add the steak and stir-fry gently until coated with the Orange Sauce. Serve immediately with a sprinkle of the diced green onion tops.

YIELD: *6 servings.* **Nutritional Facts Per Serving:** Calories 190; Total Fat 13g (Saturated Fat 2g); Cholesterol 35mg; Sodium 220mg; Total Carbohydrate 18g (Dietary Fiber 0g; Sugars 9g); Protein 2g

Dry-Fried String Beans (Gan-Bian Si-Ji-Dou) *(photo: page 77)*

Ingredients:

1 pound fresh string beans
1 teaspoon dried shrimp
1½ teaspoons Szechuan cabbage
1 green onion
2 slices fresh gingerroot, minced
2 garlic cloves, minced

Seasoning Sauce:

1 tablespoon dark soy sauce
1 teaspoon Hoisin sauce or
 sweet bean sauce
1 tablespoon rice wine or pale
 dry sherry
1½ teaspoons sugar
1½ teaspoons rice vinegar
1 teaspoon sesame oil

4 to 6 cups peanut oil for deep-frying
2 tablespoons vegetable oil
4 ounces ground pork

Preparation:

* Snap or trim the ends from the beans and cut into 3-inch pieces. Rinse the beans, pat dry and set aside.
* Soak the dried shrimp in hot water for 10 minutes, drain and chop very finely and set aside.
* Rinse the Szechuan cabbage with cold water to remove the salt and ground chili powder, drain well, chop finely and set aside.
* Dice the green onion into ¼-inch pieces, separate the white and green portions and set aside with the gingerroot and garlic.
* Prepare the Seasoning Sauce by combining the soy sauce, Hoisin sauce, rice wine, sugar, rice vinegar and sesame oil, mix well and set aside.

Procedure:

1. Heat the peanut oil for deep-frying to 375 degrees. Deep-fry the green beans about ¼ at a time until the beans are wrinkled, drain well and place on paper towels.
2. Heat a wok. Swirl the 2 tablespoons vegetable oil in the wok. Add the white of the green onion, gingerroot and garlic and stir-fry until fragrant.
3. Add the ground pork and stir-fry until cooked through and crumbly.
4. Add the shrimp and Szechuan cabbage and stir-fry for several seconds. Add the beans and the Seasoning Sauce and stir-fry briskly.
5. Sprinkle with the green onion tops and serve immediately.

Si-Ji-Dou, Four-Season Beans, are string beans that are longer than the Western string beans and are found growing in Szechuan and Hunan all year round. In this interesting dish, string beans are first deep-fried until shriveled, and then stir-fried with three complementary flavors (ground pork, Szechuan cabbage, and dried shrimp) to give the beans a rich, marvelous taste.

YIELD: 6 *servings*. **Nutritional Facts Per Serving:** Calories 190; Total Fat 16g (Saturated Fat 3g); Cholesterol 15mg; Sodium 190mg; Total Carbohydrate 8g (Dietary Fiber 3g; Sugars 3g); Protein 5g

Shark's fin is a fine delicacy to Chinese just as caviar is to Westerners. It has high nutritional value with its protein and minerals, but it is very expensive because of its rareness and elaborate preparations. The long needle-like gelatinous threads of dried cartilage from the fins of the shark are sold commercially in two forms: (1) whole body and needles or (2) shredded needles. Whole is preferred and also more expensive, requiring longer preparation and cooking. The pale ivory-colored fin is considered the best quality. Shark's fin, which is served for a special dinner or formal banquet, can be prepared in two ways: soup, or braised (also called red cooking with soy sauce). Dry shark's fin can be kept indefinitely in a can, and boiled shark's fin can be stored in the freezer.

Shark's Fin Soup (photo: page 77)

Ingredients:

2 ounces shark's fin needles
4 (¼ inch thick × 1 inch diameter) fresh gingerroot slices
1 green onion
4 dried black mushrooms
½ cup boneless chicken breast
1 tablespoon light soy sauce
1 teaspoon cornstarch
1 green onion
¼ cup bamboo shoots
½ cup ham

Thickener:
2 tablespoons lotus root or water chestnut powder
¼ cup water

2 egg whites
1 tablespoon peanut, soybean or vegetable oil
½ teaspoon salt
4 cups chicken stock
2 tablespoons rice wine or pale dry sherry
Dash each of rice vinegar, pepper and sugar
2 teaspoons sesame oil
Parsley leaves

Preparation:
- Soak the shark's fin in cold water to cover overnight. Discard any dirt or dark tough pieces from the fins, rinse and drain well.
- Fill a 2-quart saucepan ⅔ full with cold water. Add the shark's fin and 2 slices gingerroot. Bring to a boil, reduce the heat and simmer, covered, for 30 minutes. Drain the shark's fin and repeat the boiling and simmering process with fresh water, the

remaining 2 gingerroot slices and 1 green onion. Drain well. This step will eliminate any unpleasant fishy odor.
- Soak the dried black mushrooms in boiling water to cover for 15 minutes, drain and squeeze dry. Discard the stems, slice the caps into fine shreds and set aside.
- Shred the chicken breast into ⅛ × ⅛ × 1½-inch shreds, place in a bowl and mix with the light soy sauce and cornstarch and set aside.
- Shred 1 green onion (separate the white and green portions), bamboo shoots and ham into shreds the same size as the chicken and set aside.
- Prepare the Thickener by dissolving the lotus root powder in ¼ cup water and set aside.
- Beat the egg whites with cooking chopsticks until fluffy and set aside.

Procedure:
1. Heat a wok and add the peanut oil. Add the white of the green onion and stir-fry until fragrant. Add the chicken and stir-fry until the chicken turns white. Add the salt, bamboo shoots, mushrooms, shark's fin and stir-fry for several seconds.
2. Add the chicken stock and rice wine to the wok and bring to a boil. Stir in the lotus Thickener and cook until thickened, stirring constantly.
3. Add the ham and the beaten egg whites, stirring with cooking chopsticks. Turn off the heat and sprinkle with the rice vinegar, pepper, sugar, sesame oil, parsley leaves and green onion tops, mix gently and serve immediately from a tureen.

YIELD: 6 *servings*. **Nutritional Facts Per Serving:** Calories 130; Total Fat 5g (Saturated Fat 1g); Cholesterol 25mg; Sodium 740mg; Total Carbohydrate 5g (Dietary Fiber 1g); Sugars 0g); Protein 14g

Dong-An Chicken

Ingredients:

1 (2½-pound) frying chicken
2 slices fresh gingerroot
1 green onion, coarsely chopped
½ cup dried wood ear
2 green onions
2 garlic cloves
2 slices fresh gingerroot
4 red chili peppers
1 tablespoon fermented black beans
8 ounces fresh broccoli

Seasoning Sauce:

1 teaspoon hot bean sauce
1 tablespoon dark soy sauce
1 tablespoon rice wine
1 teaspoon rice vinegar
1 teaspoon sugar
1 teaspoon chili sesame oil

1 tablespoon cornstarch
2 teaspoons water
4 tablespoons vegetable oil
½ teaspoon flower pepper, crushed
1 cup reserved chicken broth

Preparation:

- Combine the chicken, 2 slices gingerroot and the green onion pieces in a saucepan. Add water to cover, bring to a boil, reduce the heat and simmer, covered, for 20 minutes or until the chicken is tender. Remove the chicken to cool. Strain and reserve the broth.
- Bone the chicken, discard the skin and bones and cut the meat into ¼ × ¾ × 1½-inch pieces and set aside.
- Soak the wood ear in boiling water to cover for 15 minutes, drain, squeeze dry and cut into ¼ × 1½-inch shreds and set aside.
- Cut the whites of the 2 green onions into ¼-inch dice and the green tops into fine 1½-inch shreds. Mince the garlic and 2 slices gingerroot. Seed the chili peppers and cut into fine shreds.
- Rinse the black beans lightly and pat dry. Cut the broccoli into pieces the size of the chicken and set aside.
- Prepare the Seasoning Sauce by mixing the hot bean sauce, soy sauce, rice wine, rice vinegar, sugar and chili sesame oil together and set aside.
- Dissolve the cornstarch in 2 teaspoons water and set aside.

Procedure:

1. Heat a wok. Add 2 tablespoons oil, swirl and add the broccoli. Stir-fry for several seconds and remove the broccoli.
2. Add the remaining 2 tablespoons oil, white of the green onions, garlic, gingerroot, flower pepper, chili peppers and black beans and stir-fry until fragrant.
3. Add the wood ear, chicken and Seasoning Sauce and stir-fry for several seconds. Return the broccoli to the wok and stir-fry for several seconds.
4. Add the reserved chicken broth, cover the wok and bring to a boil. Stir in the cornstarch mixture and cook until thickened, stirring constantly. Stir in the green onion shreds. Serve immediately.

This dish is named after Dong-An County in Hunan Province, the birthplace of the famous general Tang Shen-Chi. It was he who made this dish famous. A young chicken is first parboiled and then stir-fried with a combination of spices to produce the unique taste of Hunan.

YIELD: *6 servings.* **Nutritional Facts Per Serving:** Calories 210; Total Fat 13g (Saturated Fat 1.5g); Cholesterol 55mg; Sodium 240mg; Total Carbohydrate 6g (Dietary Fiber 0g; Sugars 1g); Protein 19g

Lovers Shrimp (photo: Front Cover and page 77)

This recipe is one of my favorite dishes. I catered it frequently for the Peking Opera Company during their visit to Washington D.C. for performances at the Kennedy Center in 1980. It is a gourmet dish with excellent taste and charming visual appeal. The name of the dish describes the romantic linkage between male and female shrimp, Coral and Crystal shrimp, swimming in the ocean of seagrass that is represented by the spinach or Chinese cabbage leaves.

Ingredients:

1 pound large fresh shrimp

Marinade:
1 egg white
$4^{1}/_{2}$ teaspoons cornstarch

White of 1 large or
    2 small green onions
2 slices fresh gingerroot

Crystal Shrimp Mix:
1 tablespoon rice wine
$1/_{2}$ teaspoon sesame oil
$1/_{2}$ teaspoon salt

Coral Shrimp Mix:
2 tablespoons ketchup
$1^{1}/_{2}$ teaspoons hot bean sauce
$1/_{2}$ teaspoon Hunan hot oil (chili oil)

4 to 6 cups peanut oil for deep-frying
4 tablespoons vegetable oil
5 to 6 ounces spinach or Chinese
    cabbage leaves
Pinch of salt

Preparation:

- Peel the shrimp, devein, rinse and pat dry. Place the shrimp in a bowl.
- Mix the egg white and cornstarch together and mix gently until the shrimp are coated. Marinate in the refrigerator for 30 minutes.
- Cut the green onion into $1/_{4}$-inch dice, mince the gingerroot and set aside.
- Prepare the Crystal Shrimp Mix by combining the rice wine, sesame oil and salt and set aside.
- Prepare the Coral Shrimp Mix by combining the ketchup, hot bean sauce and Hunan hot oil and set aside.

Procedure:

1. Heat the oil for deep-frying to 375 degrees. Deep fry the shrimp in the hot oil for 2 minutes and drain on paper towels.
2. Heat a wok. Add 2 tablespoons of the vegetable oil. Add the spinach and a pinch of salt and stir-fry for several seconds. Remove the spinach to a serving platter and place it to form a line down the center of the platter.
3. Add the remaining 2 tablespoons vegetable oil to the wok. Add the green onion and gingerroot and stir-fry until fragrant.
4. Add the shrimp and the Crystal Shrimp Mix and stir-fry briskly. Remove half the shrimp to one side of the spinach line. These are called the Crystal Shrimp.
5. Stir the Coral Shrimp Mix into the remaining shrimp in the wok and stir-fry briskly just until mixed. Place the shrimp on the other side of the spinach line. These are called the Coral Shrimp. Serve immediately.

YIELD: *6 servings.* **Nutritional Facts Per Serving:** Calories 250; Total Fat 18g (Saturated Fat 2g); Cholesterol 115mg; Sodium 460mg; Total Carbohydrate 5g (Dietary Fiber 0g; Sugars 1g); Protein 17g

Dry-Fried Shredded Beef *(photo: page 77)*

Ingredients:
1 pound top round or flank steak

Marinade:
1 tablespoon rice wine
1 teaspoon dark soy sauce
$1/2$ teaspoon baking soda

1 cup celery
$1/2$ cup carrot, peeled
2 green onions
3 garlic cloves
1 slice fresh gingerroot
4 dried red chili peppers

Seasoning Sauce:
$1/2$ teaspoon sweet bean or Hoisin
  sauce
1 tablespoon soy sauce
1 tablespoon rice wine
1 tablespoon sesame chili oil
1 tablespoon sugar
$1/2$ teaspoon rice vinegar

6 cups peanut oil for deep-frying
2 tablespoons vegetable oil

Preparation:
- The beef should be partially frozen to cut as thin as possible. Cut the beef into $1/8 \times 1/2 \times 2^{1}/2$-inch shreds and place in a bowl. Prepare the Marinade by mixing the rice wine, soy sauce and baking soda together, add to the shredded beef, mix well and set aside to marinate for 20 minutes.
- Slice the celery, carrot, and the green onion tops into $1/4 \times 1/4 \times 2$-inch shreds and set aside. Dice the whites of the green onions, mince the garlic and gingerroot and set aside.

- Cut the tips from the chili peppers, discard the seeds and cut the pods into $1/4$-inch pieces.
- Prepare the Seasoning Sauce by mixing the sweet bean sauce, soy sauce, rice wine, sesame chili oil, sugar and rice vinegar together and set aside.

Procedure:
1. Heat the oil for deep-frying to 400 degrees in a 14-inch wok. Stir the beef shreds to separate and add small amounts of the beef shreds at a time to the hot oil, stirring and separating the shreds with cooking chopsticks. Deep-fry until the shreds shrink and turn crisp and dark brown. Remove the shreds with a wire strainer and drain on paper towels.
2. Heat a wok, add the 2 tablespoons vegetable oil and swirl to coat. Add the white of the green onions, garlic, gingerroot and chili peppers and stir-fry until fragrant.
3. Add the celery, carrot and Seasoning Sauce and stir-fry until the sauce starts to thicken. Add the deep-fried beef, mix quickly, sprinkle with the green onion top shreds and serve immediately.

In Chinese cuisine, the emphasis is usually on the tenderness of the meat, but this dish is very different. The unique feature is the texture of the thin-shredded beef which tastes dry, light, crispy and chewy. Good cutting technique, to slice the beef uniformly thin, and mastery of slow, careful deep-frying in very hot oil is essential.

YIELD: *6 servings.* **Nutritional Facts Per Serving:** Calories 260; Total Fat 16g (Saturated Fat 2.5g); Cholesterol 45mg; Sodium 170mg; Total Carbohydrate 9g (Dietary Fiber 1g; Sugars 3g); Protein 19g

Honey-Glazed Ham *(photo: page 78)*

Hunan cuisine varies from fiery hot dishes to mild sweet ham. This notable Hunan banquet dish is sliced thin, steamed or baked and served with warm thin bread.

If you prefer to use an uncooked ham, prepare by scalding the whole ham in boiling water for 30 minutes. Then trim off and discard the skin and fat and steam the ham for 30 minutes. After this preparation, follow the recipe at right.

Ingredients:

1 (1½-pound) fully cooked and smoked
   boneless ham
1 teaspoon sesame oil

Sauce:
¼ cup crystal sugar, granulated sugar
   or brown sugar
½ cup honey
1 tablespoon rice wine

½ cup lotus or gingko nuts
16 white bread slices

Preparation and Procedure:

1. Trim the ham of all fat and skin. Cut the ham crosswise into ¼ × 2 × 4-inch pieces.

2. Select a deep 8-inch diameter heatproof bowl. Coat the bowl lightly with the sesame oil for easier unmolding. Arrange the ham slices decoratively in the bowl with the perfect slices at the bottom.

3. Prepare the Sauce by mixing the sugar, honey and rice wine in a small bowl and mix well. Cover the ham slices with half the mixture. Reserve the remaining mixture.

4. Place the bowl in a steamer and steam for 30 minutes. Pour off the pan juices carefully into a small saucepan and set aside.

5. Sprinkle the lotus seeds and the remaining Sauce mixture over the ham slices. Steam for 30 minutes longer.

6. Place a plate over the bowl and invert carefully to unmold the ham.

7. Heat the pan juices in the saucepan and pour over the ham.

8. Cut the crusts from the bread. The slices should be ½ inch thick and about 2 × 4-inch pieces. Make a cut across the center of the rectangle to score but do not cut through.

9. Steam the bread slices very briefly to soften and warm. Place the ham and lotus nuts in the warm bread and eat like a sandwich.

YIELD: 6 *servings.* **Nutritional Facts Per Serving:** Calories 320; Total Fat 6g (Saturated Fat 2g); Cholesterol 60mg; Sodium 1510mg; Total Carbohydrate 36g (Dietary Fiber 0g; Sugars 32g); Protein 29g

Minced Chicken in Lettuce Bowls (photo: page 78)

Ingredients:

16 large iceberg lettuce leaves
4 small or 2 large dried black
    mushrooms
1 teaspoon dried shrimp
12 ounces boneless skinless
    chicken breast
2 slices fresh gingerroot
1 medium green bell pepper
2 tablespoons bamboo shoots
4 ounces ground pork or diced ham
2 green onions
1 teaspoon hot bean sauce
1 teaspoon Hoisin sauce or
    sweet bean sauce
2 tablespoons soy sauce
1 tablespoon rice wine or pale
    dry sherry
1 1/2 teaspoons sugar
1 teaspoon sesame chili oil
4 to 6 cups peanut oil for deep-frying
1 ounce rice noodles
2 tablespoons vegetable oil
2 tablespoons roasted peanuts, finely
    crushed

Preparation:

- Use kitchen scissors to trim the lettuce leaves into circles and shape into bowls, using 2 lettuce leaves for each bowl. Arrange the bowls on a tray and keep chilled.
- Soak the black mushrooms and dried shrimp in boiling water to cover for 15 minutes. Drain, reserving the soaking liquid. Squeeze the mushrooms dry, discard the stems and chop the caps. Pat the shrimp dry and chop very finely.
- Mince the chicken and gingerroot and set aside.

- Discard the seeds and membranes from the green pepper. Cut the green pepper, bamboo shoots, pork and the white and green tops of the green onions into 1/4-inch dice and set aside.
- Combine the hot bean sauce and Hoisin sauce and set aside. Combine the soy sauce, rice wine, sugar, sesame chili oil and the reserved mushroom soaking liquid and set aside.

Procedure:

1. Heat the oil for deep-frying to 400 degrees. Add 1/4 of the rice noodles at a time to the hot oil. Remove the noodles quickly as they puff instantly, drain on paper towels, crush and set aside.

2. Heat a wok. Swirl 2 tablespoons oil in the wok. Add the white of the green onions and the gingerroot and stir-fry until fragrant. Add the chicken, pork and hot bean sauce mixture and stir-fry until cooked through.

3. Add the mushrooms, shrimp, bamboo shoots, green pepper and the soy sauce mixture and stir-fry until well mixed.

4. Divide the crushed peanuts and rice noodles among the lettuce bowls. Add the chicken mixture, sprinkle with the green onion tops and serve immediately. Use fingers to wrap the chicken in the lettuce leaves and eat.

This elegant and tasty dish originated in the neighboring province of Canton, but it has long been a Hunan specialty by adding hot spices. In the old classic version, dove (squab) or quail was used. The dish can be served as an appetizer or a main course.

YIELD: *6 servings.* **Nutritional Facts Per Serving:** Calories 250; Total Fat 19g (Saturated Fat 3g); Cholesterol 45mg; Sodium 100mg; Total Carbohydrate 6g (Dietary Fiber 1g; Sugars 2g); Protein 18g

Chinese Onion Cake (photo: page 78)

This famous classic Chinese snack can be served with soybean milk for breakfast, or as an appetizer at a banquet. The delicious flaky pastry that looks like crêpes is pan-fried to a golden crispy texture with aromatic green onion flavor. For richer onion cakes, brush 2 beaten eggs on the top of the cakes in addition to the shortening, green onion, oil and salt before pan-frying. The finished onion cakes can be prepared and kept in a preheated warm oven until serving time.

Ingredients:

2 cups all-purpose flour
^{2}/$_3$ cup boiling water
Cornstarch
3 tablespoons vegetable shortening
1 tablespoon Hunan hot oil (chili oil)
3 tablespoons finely chopped green onion
^{1}/$_2$ teaspoon salt
6 tablespoons vegetable oil

Preparation:

- Place the flour in a bowl. Add the boiling water and mix with cooking chopsticks until the mixture clings together. Turn the mixture onto a surface lightly dusted with cornstarch and knead until smooth. Cover with a warm moist towel and let rest for 30 minutes.

Procedure:

1. Knead the dough for 3 minutes and shape into a 1-inch diameter rope. Cut into 6 portions.
2. Press each portion flat with the palm of the hand and roll into a thin 8-inch round cake.
3. Spread the top of the cake with 1^1/$_2$ teaspoons shortening, sprinkle with ^{1}/$_2$ teaspoon Hunan oil, 1^1/$_2$ teaspoons green onion and a pinch of salt. Roll up as for a jelly roll, twist the roll into a spiral, press flat and roll to ^{1}/$_4$-inch thickness.
4. Heat a wok over medium heat. Add 2 tablespoons of the vegetable oil and pan-fry on both sides until light brown and crispy.
5. Repeat the rolling and pan-frying procedure with the remaining ingredients. Stack the onion cakes on a warm plate, cut into fourths and keep covered with a dry towel to keep warm and crisp.

YIELD: *6 servings.* **Nutritional Facts Per Serving:** Calories 310; Total Fat 18g (Saturated Fat 3g); Cholesterol 0mg; Sodium 200mg; Total Carbohydrate 32g (Dietary Fiber 0g; Sugars 0g); Protein 4g

White Jade Vegetable Rolls

Ingredients:

12 large leaves Napa cabbage
1 tablespoon salt
Pinch of salt
10 ounces fresh spinach
2 fresh red chili peppers
1 tablespoon white sesame seeds

Dipping Sauce:
1 tablespoon light soy sauce
1 teaspoon hot bean sauce
1 teaspoon fermented black beans
2 tablespoons rice vinegar
2 tablespoons sugar
2 teaspoons sesame oil
1 teaspoon Hunan hot oil (chili oil)

Preparation:

- Rinse the cabbage leaves, cut off and discard the hard stems, rub the tablespoon of salt over the surface of the leaves and place the leaves in a pan. Place a heavy weight on the leaves and let stand for 30 minutes to soften.
- Rinse the cabbage leaves under cool running water and drain well.
- Bring a generous amount of water with a pinch of salt to a boil in a saucepan. Add the spinach and blanch for a minute or two. Drain well and set aside to cool. Divide the spinach into 6 portions.

- Cut the ends from the chili peppers, tap the seeds out, slice the pods into rings and set aside.
- Stir-fry the sesame seeds in a preheated dry wok over low heat until fragrant. (If the sesame seeds have been toasted, there is no need to stir-fry.)
- Prepare the Dipping Sauce by combining the soy sauce, hot bean sauce, black beans, rice vinegar, sugar, sesame oil and Hunan hot oil in a bowl or saucepan and mix well. Serve the sauce cold or heat to desired temperature.

Procedure:

1. Place a double layer of cabbage leaves on a bamboo sushi mat. Add one portion of the spinach and roll up as for a jelly roll, pressing tightly while rolling and allowing any liquid to drain through the bamboo. Repeat until all the cabbage and spinach are used.
2. Cut the rolls into 1-inch slices and arrange cut side up on a serving platter.
3. Arrange the chili pepper rings on the rolls and sprinkle with the sesame seeds.
4. Pour the Dipping Sauce over the rolls just before serving.

These vegetable rolls are simple to prepare, yet beautiful, elegant, and nutritious. The soft spinach fillings in the center are tightly wrapped with layers of crisp Napa (Chinese) cabbage. The contrast in textures of these vegetables gives a sensational bite, and the color combination of pale yellow and deep green gives the natural look of precious jade.

YIELD: 6 *servings*. **Nutritional Facts Per Serving:** Calories 50; Total Fat 2.5g (Saturated Fat 0g); Cholesterol 0mg; Sodium 480mg; Total Carbohydrate 5g (Dietary Fiber 1g; Sugars 3g); Protein 2g

Tea-Smoked Duck *(photo: page 78)*

This is one of the most celebrated Hunan and Szechuan banquet dishes. The unique flavor of the duck is a result of smoke from burning camphor wood chips, tea, sugar and rice. The taste is subtle and enticingly exotic. If camphor wood chips are not available, use pine needles.

Ingredients:

1 (4$\frac{1}{2}$- to 5-pound) duck

Marinade:
2 green onions
3 tablespoons dark soy sauce
1 tablespoon rice wine or pale
    dry sherry
4 slices fresh gingerroot, minced
5 star anise, crushed
1 tablespoon Szechuan flower pepper,
    crushed
1 tablespoon honey
Dash of salt

4 tablespoons black tea leaves
    (Yunnan)
3 tablespoons brown sugar
3 tablespoons rice
Several camphor wood chips or
    pine needles
6 cups peanut oil for deep-frying

Preparation:

- Rinse the duck inside and out and pat dry.
- Prepare the Marinade by cutting the green onions into $\frac{1}{4}$-inch dice and mixing with the soy sauce, rice wine, gingerroot, star anise, flower pepper, honey and salt.
- Rub the Marinade over the duck inside and outside and marinate in the refrigerator for 4 hours. (For a stronger flavored duck, marinate for 8 hours to overnight in the refrigerator.)
- Place the duck on a rack in a steamer and steam for 1 hour.
- Line a wok with several layers of aluminum foil to prevent the caramelized sugar from sticking to the wok and burning.

Procedure:

1. Place the tea leaves, brown sugar, rice and camphor chips in the foil-lined wok. Place the steamed duck, breast side up, on a rack over the tea mixture. Cover the wok, turn the heat under the wok on high and smoke for 5 minutes.

2. Turn off the heat and let stand for 3 minutes. Turn the heat to high for 5 minutes, turn off the heat and let stand for 3 minutes. Remove the duck to cool and discard the smoking materials.

3. Heat the oil for deep-frying to 350 degrees. Cut the duck into halves and deep-fry the duck until it turns a deep coffee brown color.

4. Cut the duck into 2½-inch pieces and reassemble into the original duck shape on a serving platter.

5. Serve the duck with Steamed Lotus Leaf Buns (page 123), Chinese Onion Cake (page 138), and Hoisin sauce or flower pepper salt (see sidebar, page 125).

YIELD: 6 *servings*. **Nutritional Facts Per Serving:** Calories 390; Total Fat 24g; (Saturated Fat 7g); Cholesterol 135mg; Sodium 400mg; Total Carbohydrate 5g (Dietary Fiber 0g; Sugars 3g); Protein 36g

Vegetarian Cuisine

Popular Vegetarian Dishes

INTRODUCTION: History and Philosophy / Characteristics and Nutritional Requirements / Ingredients

Vegetarian Cuisine

Chinese vegetarianism has a long history dating back to the sixth century B.C. It was derived from the two philosophical ideologies of Taoism and Confucianism during the middle of the Chou Dynasty (1122–225 B.C.). The word, *Tao*, means *The Way*. The Taoists seek life in a simple and natural way. They believe that the whole universe is made up of two opposite, interlocking forces, Yin (negative, weak, feminine, dark, cold) and Yang (positive, strong, masculine, light, hot) coexisting in a balancing state of flux. Peace, happiness, and harmony can be maintained so long as these two interdependent matters are in balance. Taoism philosophy on good health is to eat a vegetarian diet and to elevate the well-being of the mind, body, and spirit by meditation.

Confucius, a great philosopher, educator, and passionate gourmet, taught: "Harmony is the essential factor in life." Harmony brings the family together, and builds a great society. In Chinese culinary art, the harmonious mixture in a dish is desired. The last deriving and influencing factors were furnished by Buddhism, introduced from India into China during the reign of the Han Emperor Ming (57–75 A.D.). Opening the passages to the western border started a rapid rise of Buddhist temples in China. The trade brought in many foreign fruits and vegetables. The code of ahimsa (no injury) reinforced vegetarianism among the Buddhists until the present time.

In recent years, more people are becoming vegetarians for health reasons. I was very surprised to see many vegetarian restaurants opened in Taipei on my visit home during the early 1990s. The problem of eating high cholesterol and high calorie foods has been the concern of modern Taiwanese, because it can lead to illnesses such as heart disease, stroke, diabetes, and cancer. Weight control, by eating light and healthy food, is of the utmost importance. Vegetarian foods are prepared only from materials of plant origin. They are rich in fiber which has the ability of speeding wastes through the intestines, thus lessening the chances of cancer. The fibrous matter can change the characteristics of the bacteria in the intestines and suppress carcinogenic substances. A vegetarian diet can also reduce the concentration of cholesterol and glycerides in the blood thus preventing cardiovascular diseases.

Characteristics and Nutritional Requirements

Chinese vegetarianism is deeply rooted in Buddhist and Taoist traditions. Five pungent foods (garlic, onion, leek, chive, and scallion) cannot be used in cooking, because they give one's body a bad odor. According to its doctrine: "A person seeks to purify his body and mind through Buddhism, has to keep himself in a clean state by eating pure foods." This is the main difference between Chinese and other vegetarian cuisines. Buddha advocates mercy, equality, and salvation. Mercy is the main reason that Chinese vegetarians abstain from eating the flesh of living animals, although eggs are permitted for use in cooking.

Chinese vegetarian cuisine has existed for 2000 years, so it is a very advanced form of art and science combined. The artistic presentation, the good taste of harmonious mixture, the texture of vegetables and nutritional value are all emphasized in making an authentic vegetarian dish. Vegetarians can achieve greater longevity because of the vegetarian diet which is low in fat, high in dietary fiber and complex carbohydrates. One of the main concerns with a vegetarian diet should be an adequate intake of protein which provides energy and maintains growth of body tissue. Protein consists of twenty-two building blocks called amino acids. Eight essential amino acids cannot be made by our bodies, and must come from the food that we eat. Individual vegetable foods do not contain all essential amino acids; therefore, a variety of plant food is necessary to make a complete protein.

Soy protein is nutritionally superior to other vegetable proteins, because it contains good supplies of essential amino acids (except that it is slightly deficient in cystine and methionine). The principle of the Chinese vegetarian diet is to combine soybean foods and rice. Rice is rich in methionine, but deficient in lysine which can be supplemented by soybeans. Soybeans, and the byproducts processed in many forms, are important ingredients for Chinese vegetarian cooking. Soybeans are very rich in protein, carbohydrate, and other nutrients including calcium, iron, potassium, vitamins A, B1, B2, C, and E. Another Chinese vegetarian protein, Mein-qing (gluten extracted from flour dough), was discovered by Han Chinese in the first century A.D. Special herbs such as Ginseng, Silver Ears, Angelica, and Reishi Mushrooms have been used as medicinal foods in cooking by rich Chinese for many centuries.

Ingredients of Chinese Vegetarianism

Rice and Rice Products

Long Grain White Rice is suitable for making Chinese steamed rice. *Jasmine Rice* is a fine quality, extra-long grain rice. *Sushi Rice* is a medium round-grain rice and is a little bit moist and glutinous in nature. Japanese prefer it for making steamed rice and sushi. *Sweet Rice* (Glutinous Rice) is sticky and has a natural sweet taste, suitable for making dim-sum, oriental cakes and sweets. It is used for making Mirin, the Japanese sweet rice cooking wine.

Brown rice, unlike white rice, is unpolished. Only the hull has been removed. The vital structure of its rice grain, the germ and the bran, remains. Therefore, it is live and nutritious. It can be used for rice stuffing or plain steamed rice. Steamed Brown Rice requires more water to cook the rice. A touch of sesame oil will give fragrance and keep brown rice moist.

Black rice is long grain rice which is grown popularly in Southeast Asia. It is glutinous when cooked and often used in making sweet desserts. It should be soaked for about two hours before cooking.

Red rice has a taste similar to Brown Rice and is glutinous in nature. It is not a highly regarded grain. It should be soaked for two hours before cooking.

Rice flour (Mi-Fun) is made commercially from low-grade rice with a high proportion of millet, which is known as little rice (Xiao-Mi). The grain is soaked in water for two days, then ground with water. The thick paste is poured into fine cheesecloth sacks which are hung up to drain off the liquid. The wet flour is then spread out on a mat to be sun-dried before being packaged for sale. Rice flour can be used as a thickening starch, or to prepare a batter for coating food before deep-frying or steaming. Rice flour is an ingredient for making rice cakes.

Rice Noodles (Mi-Fun) are also called Rice Sticks. The better grade rice is used for making rice noodles which are manufactured commercially. The process involves soaking the rice in water for two days, then grinding with water into a thick paste. The paste is boiled, then kneaded with raw rice flour into a stiff dough. The dough is then put through a cutting press to shape into very fine, long noodles. Rice sticks are sun-dried before packaging for sale. The best quality rice noodles are made in Taiwan.

Rice paper is made of rice flour, water, and salt. It is rolled out paper-thin by a machine and sun-dried before packaging for sale. Rice papers are used for wrapping Taiwanese or Vietnamese egg rolls. Dip rice paper wrappers in water for one to two minutes before use.

Wheat Flour

Wheat gluten (Mein-Chin) is known as Mock or Vegetarian Meat. The gluten is a wheat flour and water dough that has been soaked and kneaded in water to rinse out the starch. The remaining product is spongy and porous with firm texture and a strong flavor. It can be used as vegetarian duck, mock chicken, or abalone.

Beans and Sprouting Vegetables

Mung Beans or Green Beans are small, round, green-colored beans. They are used to make sweet bean paste for the filling in moon cakes, and are grown in water to produce bean sprouts.

Bean Sprouts are very nutritious and low in calories. Serve hot by preparing as stir-fry, or cold as in salads.

Bean Theads are called Fensi or Saifun which means very thin noodles, Chinese vermicelli. They are made of mung bean starch.

Soybeans

Soybeans and soybean products have been regarded as vegetarian meats because of their high protein value. There are black, yellow, green, and white soybeans.

Soybean Sprouts are twice as long as those of mung beans; the color of the bean is yellow. Do not eat the sprouts raw, they are slightly toxic. Because of the high protein and fat content, Soybean Sprouts are an important ingredient for making vegetarian soup stock.

Soy Milk is a milk-like product made when soybeans are soaked overnight in water, then ground with a food grinder. After an anti-foaming agent has been added, the mixture is thoroughly heated by means of steam from a boiler. The batch is then filtered to give soy milk.

Soybean Cheese is made when the film which forms on the surface of heated soy milk is lifted and dried. Heat and pressure are applied to bind many layers of film and become soybean cheese (called Yuba in Japanese) which consists largely of protein and oil. The following products of Yuba (soybean cheese), called Imitation Meats, can be processed to resemble chicken, duck, or abalone meats in flavor and texture, then packed into a can or frozen for sale commercially.

Soybean Sticks are Yuba cut into long sticks, covered with baking soda, allowed to stand for an hour, and then deep-fried into crispy sticks.

Soybean Buns are made by stacking many layers of Yuba together, shaping to resemble a 3-inch square pouch, and then steaming.

Soybean Rolls are made by rolling Yuba into long sticks about one inch in diameter and steaming. Use as Vegetarian Sausage in cooking.

Tofu or Dou-fu (Bean Curd) forms when soy milk and calcium sulfate is heated at 70 degrees C (158 degrees F) until coagulated, then stirred vigorously to separate the curd and whey. The curds are molded into a wooden or perforated aluminum box, covered with cheesecloth and a bamboo mat, and then pressed with a weight to form a block.

Pressed Bean Curd is the firm tofu resulting when the weight on the tofu removes the water completely. Spiced Bean Curd is cooked in black tea, a pinch of sugar, and five fragrant spices until the tofu is colored brown. Because of its dehydrated, hard texture, this bean curd is good to cut into shreds and stir-fry with vegetables.

Bean Curd Skin results when the thin film on the surface of heated soy milk is lifted and toasted dry over a charcoal fire. It is used in making vegetarian egg rolls.

Soy Flour is made from ground, dried soybeans and is rich in high-quality protein and other nutrients. It can be used in baked goods. Store in a freezer or refrigerator for it goes rancid quickly.

Soybean Oil is a richer and heavier oil than others. It can retain high temperatures, and is suitable for use in deep-frying.

Fermented Soybean Products

Miso is a fermented thick soybean paste that is an essential condiment in Chinese and Japanese cooking. It has an earthy and full-bodied flavor. Miso is available in the East in different textures, chunky and smooth, but only the smooth one is found in the West. White and Dark Miso are made of white and dark soybeans. Miso is made from soybeans, rice or barley, salt and mold culture, *aspergillus oryzae*, and placed in wooden kegs to ferment. The mixture is aged for about two years.

Soy Sauce is the most important condiment in Chinese and Japanese cooking. A naturally brewed soy sauce takes twelve to eighteen months of aging or fermenting in the old traditional method. The modern method using controlled temperature and humidity can speed up the production. Defatted soybeans are steamed, mixed with roasted, crushed wheat and inoculated with koji (*aspergillus oryzae*) and salted water for fermentation. About six months later, the raw soy sauce residue is pressed out, then pasteurized to intensify the color and aroma into a refined soy sauce called Shoyu in Japanese. Tamari Shoyu like Chinese soy sauce (Chian-You) is made of soybeans, koji, and salted water; the crushed wheat is omitted.

Fermented Black Beans (Douchi) are cooked soybeans fermented in the same way as in soy sauce. The fermented beans are sun-dried and packaged in plastic bags for commercial sale. The odor is strong. Fermented black beans can be kept in a refrigerator indefinitely. Rinse the salt coating before use. Used sparingly, it can enhance meat or seafood dishes with smoky, savory, and aromatic flavor.

Natto are sticky fermented whole soybeans. They are wrapped in a small straw package and sold in Japanese markets. The soybeans are soaked and steamed until soft, inoculated with the bacteria *bacillus natto*, and held at 104 degrees C in a humid environment for 24 hours for fermentation. Natto are soft and highly digestible because the soybeans' complex protein molecules are broken down by the bacteria during fermentation (to contain 16.5 percent protein) plus they are rich in vitamin B1.

Vegetables

Ginger is a tonic giving the body downward moving energy that can settle the stomach. It is a very popular seasoning used in Chinese and Japanese cuisine. Stem Ginger is the young variety which has smooth, clear yellowish skin and pink buds.

Taro is a starchy tuber produced in Taiwan, Canton, and other tropical parts of Asia. It has a distinct appearance compared to the other root vegetables with brown hairy skin and dark rings at regular intervals; thick roots emerge at irregular intervals. When cut, the white flesh is flecked with purple. Taros are heavy and dense, of oval shape but varying size. The two varieties are Betel-Nut Taro (Ping-Long Taro) which is large, and Red-Budded Taro (Hong-Yia Taro), which is one to two inches in diameter with a pink shoot emerging from one end. Taro has a high level of potassium and vitamins C and E. It should always be cooked, either steamed or deep-fried.

Sweet Potato or *Yam* is a tuber commonly used in the West, therefore its appearance and use should be familiar to everyone.

Lotus Roots, which are sold dried, are strings of sausage-shaped rhizomes showing air channels in the cross-section slices. The root has a mild sweet taste and must be soaked in warm water before cooking. The medicinal value is good circulation. The edible leaves are used for wrapping sticky rice (Dim-sum).

Water Chestnuts have been peeled, precooked, and imported. Use what is needed and freeze the rest, adding fresh cold water to cover. They have a mild sweet taste and crunchy texture, and are good to stir-fry with meat and vegetables.

Oriental Radish (Daikon) is large and cylindrical with smooth skin and alabaster color. It is a very nutritious, cooling, and detoxifying vegetable with the ability to dissolve internal mucous. It is good for controlling the fever of a cold and helps digestion in the body. It can be added to salads, soups, or braised dishes.

Chinese Cabbages are of several varieties: Bok-Choi (Cantonese White Cabbage with dark green leaves), Celery Cabbage (Peking Cabbage), Napa Cabbage, Shanghai Cabbage (Spoon Cabbage), Flowering Cabbage, and Water Spinach.

Crispy Nuts

These nuts are usually served at the beginning of a Chinese banquet as an appetizer.

Ingredients:

    3 cups unsalted peanuts, cashews
        or walnuts
    3 cups water
    1 cup sugar
    6 cups peanut or soybean oil for

Procedure:

1. Combine the nuts, water and sugar in a 3-quart saucepan. Bring the mixture to a boil, stirring until the sugar is dissolved completely. Reduce the heat and simmer for 8 minutes. Drain well.

2. Heat the oil for deep-frying to 350 degrees. Add the nuts and deep-fry for 5 minutes or until golden brown. (Reduce the heat slightly if necessary to avoid burning.) Drain the nuts on paper towels. The nuts will become light in weight (because the water will be extracted by the deep-frying process) and will be very crispy when cool.

YIELD: 10 *servings.* **Nutritional Facts Per Serving:** Calories 370; Total Fat 26g (Saturated Fat 4g); Cholesterol 0mg; Sodium 0mg; Total Carbohydrate 29g (Dietary Fiber 4g; Sugars 20g); Protein 10g

Dan-Dan Mein (photo: page 76)

Ingredients:
Sauce:
    2 tablespoons sesame paste
    4¹/₂ tablespoons soy sauce
    1 tablespoon chili oil
    2 teaspoons sugar
    2 teaspoons hot bean sauce
    2 teaspoons rice vinegar
    1 teaspoon minced fresh gingerroot
    ¹/₄ teaspoon finely crushed flower
        pepper

    1 teaspoon salt
    12 ounces Chinese Lo-Mein noodles
    2 teaspoons sesame oil
    Fresh coriander or parsley

Preparation:
• Combine the Sauce ingredients in a small bowl, mix well and set aside.

• Fill a 3-quart saucepan half full with water. Bring the water to a boil and add the salt.

Procedure:

1. Add the noodles to the boiling water and stir to separate the noodles. Cook for 5 minutes or until the noodles are soft.

2. Pour the noodles into a sieve or strainer and rinse under cold running water to stop the cooking and firm the noodles. Spread the noodles on a platter. Drizzle the sesame oil over the noodles and toss to mix.

3. Pour the Sauce over the noodles and toss to mix. Garnish with the coriander or parsley and serve hot or cold.

YIELD: *6 servings.* **Nutritional Facts Per Serving:** Calories 130; Total Fat 7g (Saturated Fat 1g); Cholesterol 0mg; Sodium 280mg; Total Carbohydrate 16g (Dietary Fiber 0g; Sugars 1g); Protein 4g

Dan-Dan Mein originated in Szechuan Province. It is often sold at a stand or stall called Dan-Dan. Much of the unique flavor comes from the sesame paste which is very thick and heavy beneath a layer of soybean oil in the jar. Be sure to mix the paste with the oil very well before spooning into the sauce mixture.

Soybean Curd Roll with Eggplant *(photo: Back Cover)*

Ingredients:

    2 (12- to 18-inch) round soybean
        curd skins
    1 (1-pound) eggplant
    4 ounces carrot
    ¼ cup blanched peanuts

Sealing Paste:
1 egg, beaten
1 tablespoon all-purpose flour

4 to 6 cups peanut oil for deep-frying
4 sheets Nori (Japanese roasted
    seaweed)
3 tablespoons Satay sauce

Preparation:

- Cut each of the soybean curd skins into halves and set aside.
- Peel the eggplant and cut into ½ × ¾ × 2-inch sticks. Peel the carrot and cut into ¼ × ¼ × 2-inch sticks.
- Grind the peanuts into powder and set aside.
- Prepare the Sealing Paste by beating the egg in a small bowl and blending in the flour until smooth.

Procedure:

1. Heat the oil for deep-frying to 375 degrees. Deep-fry the carrot sticks for several seconds until soft and remove to paper towels to drain. Deep-fry the eggplant sticks in about 3 batches for several seconds until soft. Remove the eggplant with a mesh-wire strainer, press with a spatula and finish draining on paper towels in a colander.

2. Place one of the soybean curd pieces on a work surface, rub a portion of the Sealing Paste over the top. Center a Nori sheet in the center and layer strips of the fried eggplant and carrot in rows on the Nori. Sprinkle with 1 tablespoon of the peanut powder and spread 2 teaspoons of the Satay sauce over the vegetables.

3. Fold the lower edge of the soybean curd skin over the filling, roll up one turn, fold in the ends of the soybean curd skin and roll up tightly. Brush the edge with the Sealing Paste and press to seal. Repeat with the remaining ingredients.

4. Deep-fry the rolls in 375-degree hot oil until crisp. Cut each of the rolls into 8 pieces, arrange on a serving platter and garnish with parsley, lettuce and tomato. Serve immediately.

YIELD: *6 servings.* **Nutritional Facts Per Serving:** Calories 130; Total Fat 5g (Saturated Fat 1g); Cholesterol 20mg; Sodium 280mg; Total Carbohydrate 13g (Dietary Fiber 3g; Sugars 3g); Protein 12g

Vegetarian Steak (photo: page 79)

Ingredients:

    4 dried black mushrooms
    10 tiger lily buds (golden needles)
    8 ounces soybean curd buns
        (or soybean curd pack)
    8 slices water chestnut

Seasoning Mix:

$^1/_2$ teaspoon five-spice powder
1 tablespoon Satay sauce (Southeast
    Asian soy and sugar-flavored
    peanut sauce)
1 tablespoon soy sauce
1 teaspoon sugar
$^1/_2$ teaspoon salt

1 egg, beaten
$^1/_2$ cup sweet potato powder
$^1/_4$ cup cornstarch
$^1/_2$ cup bread crumbs

Dipping Sauce:

$^1/_4$ cup ketchup
$1^1/_2$ teaspoons soy sauce
1 tablespoon Hoisin sauce
1 teaspoon sesame chili oil
$1^1/_2$ teaspoons gourmet rice vinegar

4 to 6 cups peanut or soybean oil for
    deep-frying
Tomato and lettuce

Preparation:

- Soak the mushrooms and tiger lily buds in boiling water to cover for 15 minutes. Drain and squeeze dry, discard the mushroom stems and chop the mushroom caps and tiger lily buds finely and place in a bowl.
- Rinse the soybean curd buns, pat dry, chop and add to the bowl. Chop the water chestnuts and add to the bowl.

- Prepare the Seasoning Mix by mixing the five-spice powder, Satay sauce, 1 tablespoon soy sauce, sugar and salt together and add to the bowl.
- Add the egg and the sweet potato powder and mix well.
- Mix the cornstarch and bread crumbs together and set aside.
- Prepare the Dipping Sauce by mixing the ketchup, $1^1/_2$ teaspoons soy sauce, Hoisin sauce, sesame chili oil and rice vinegar together and set aside.

Procedure:

1. Spread the soybean curd mixture evenly in a 9×9-inch baking dish. Bring about 1 inch of water to a boil in the bottom pan of a steamer. Place the baking dish in a steamer rack over the boiling water and steam, covered, for 10 minutes. Let stand until cooled completely.

2. Cut the steamed vegetarian steak into $3 \times 4^1/_2$-inch pieces and lift carefully from the dish with a spatula. Coat on all sides with the cornstarch and bread crumb mixture.

3. Heat the peanut oil to 375 degrees. Slide the vegetarian steak into the hot oil carefully and deep-fry until golden and crispy. Drain on paper towels, arrange on a serving platter and garnish with tomato and lettuce. Serve immediately with the Dipping Sauce.

YIELD: 6 *servings*. **Nutritional Facts Per Serving:** Calories 190; Total Fat 10g (Saturated Fat 1.5g); Cholesterol 35mg; Sodium 310mg; Total Carbohydrate 21g (Dietary Fiber 2g; Sugars 1g); Protein 6g

Stuffed Bean Curd in Brown Sauce *(photo: page 79)*

Ingredients:

1 pound firm tofu
1 tablespoon dried black mushroom
1 tablespoon chopped carrot
1 tablespoon chopped celery
1½ teaspoons cornstarch
1 tablespoon water
3 tablespoons cornstarch

Brown Sauce:

1 tablespoon Hoisin sauce
1 teaspoon sugar
1 teaspoon sesame oil
1 teaspoon soy sauce
1 cup water

1 teaspoon cornstarch
1 tablespoon water
4 cups peanut oil for deep-frying
2 tablespoons vegetable oil
2 slices fresh gingerroot, minced

Preparation:

- Cut the tofu into four 1-inch-thick 2 × 4-inch rectangles. Cut each rectangle into 2 triangles.
- Scoop out the center of each triangle to make a hollow about ½ inch in diameter and ¼ inch deep.
- Soak the black mushroom in boiling water to cover for 15 minutes. Drain, squeeze dry, discard stem and chop the cap. Combine with the carrot and celery and stuff into the tofu.
- Blend 1½ teaspoons cornstarch with 1 tablespoon water to make a paste. Moisten the tofu and the edge of the filling with about ½ teaspoon of the paste and press tightly to seal filling and tofu together.

- Coat the stuffed tofu triangles with the 3 tablespoons cornstarch.
- Prepare the Brown Sauce by mixing the Hoisin sauce, sugar, sesame oil, soy sauce and 1 cup water and set aside.
- Dissolve the 1 teaspoon cornstarch in 1 tablespoon water and set aside.

Procedure:

1. Heat the oil for deep-frying to 375 degrees. Add the tofu triangles and deep fry until light brown and crispy and drain on paper towels.
2. Heat a wok. Add 2 tablespoons oil and the gingerroot and stir-fry until fragrant. Add the tofu triangles with the stuffing side up. Add the Brown Sauce and mix gently. Cover the wok and let steam for several minutes to flavor the tofu.
3. Bring the sauce to a boil and stir in the 1 teaspoon cornstarch dissolved in 1 tablespoon water. Cook until thickened, stirring constantly. Serve immediately.

YIELD: *6 servings.* **Nutritional Facts Per Serving:** Calories 220; Total Fat 17g (Saturated Fat 2g); Cholesterol 0mg; Sodium 40mg; Total Carbohydrate 9g (Dietary Fiber 2g; Sugars 1g); Protein 12g

Vegetarian Fish in Hot Bean Sauce *(photo: page 76)*

Ingredients:

1 recipe Vegetarian Fish (page 155)

Hot Bean Sauce:
1¹/₂ teaspoons hot bean sauce
1¹/₂ teaspoons Hoisin sauce
¹/₂ teaspoon salt
2 teaspoons chili oil
1 tablespoon sugar
1 tablespoon dark soy sauce
1 tablespoon rice vinegar
3 tablespoons ketchup
1 cup water

1 tablespoon cornstarch
2 tablespoons water
1 tablespoon vegetable oil
1 teaspoon minced fresh gingerroot

Preparation:

- Prepare a recipe of the Vegetarian Fish.
- Prepare the Hot Bean Sauce mixture by combining the hot bean sauce, Hoisin sauce, salt, chili oil, sugar, soy sauce, rice vinegar, ketchup and 1 cup water in a small bowl, mix well and set aside.
- Dissolve the cornstarch in 2 tablespoons water and set aside.

Procedure:

1. Heat a wok. Add the vegetable oil and minced gingerroot and stir-fry until fragrant.
2. Add the Hot Bean Sauce mixture and mix well. Bring to a boil, stirring constantly. Stir the cornstarch mixture into the wok and cook until thickened, stirring constantly.
3. Place the Vegetarian Fish on a serving platter. Cut several slashes on the fish body and garnish with lettuce and carrot decorations. Pour the boiling hot sauce over the Vegetarian Fish and serve immediately.

YIELD: *6 servings.* **Nutritional Facts Per Serving:** Calories 240; Total Fat 12g (Saturated Fat 1g); Cholesterol 0mg; Sodium 560mg; Total Carbohydrate 20g (Dietary Fiber 5g; Sugars 6g); Protein 18g

Vegetarian Fish

Ingredients:

1 pound frozen bean curd pocket,
    thawed
1 (4-ounce) can oyster mushrooms
    (enoki), drained
2 tablespoons water chestnuts

Flavoring Mixture:

1 tablespoon cornstarch
$1\frac{1}{2}$ teaspoons sesame oil
$\frac{1}{2}$ teaspoon salt
$\frac{1}{2}$ teaspoon sugar
Dash of white or black pepper

Sealing Paste:

2 tablespoons all-purpose flour
2 tablespoons water

2 (12-inch) round bean curd sheets
    or skins
1 egg, beaten
2 sheets Nori (dry roasted seaweed
    sheets)
4 to 6 cups peanut oil for deep-frying

Preparation:

- Chop the bean curd pocket, mushrooms and water chestnuts, combine the chopped ingredients and chop again very fine and place in a bowl.
- Prepare the Flavoring Mixture by mixing the 1 tablespoon cornstarch, sesame oil, salt, sugar and pepper together, add to the bean curd mixture and mix well with cooking chopsticks.
- Prepare the Sealing Paste by blending the flour and water in a small bowl.
- Place the bean curd sheets on the work surface. Rub a portion of the egg over the sheets and place a sheet of Nori in the center of each bean curd sheet.

- Add the remaining beaten egg to the chopped bean curd mixture, mixing well. Spread the mixture over the Nori leaving a 1-inch margin on all sides of the Nori. (See illustration below.)
- Fold the lower edge of the bean curd sheet over the filling, fold the sides toward the center and roll up to form a pouch about 3×6-inches. Moisten the edges with Sealing Paste and press to seal. Repeat with the remaining ingredients to make 2 pouches.

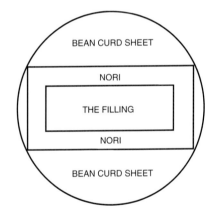

Procedure:

1. Oil a steamplate lightly. Place the bean curd pouches on the steamplate. Fill the steamer bottom pan half full with water and bring to a boil. Place the plate in the steamer and steam for 25 minutes. Place the pouches on a paper towel. Let stand until the pouches are cool and dry to the touch.
2. Heat the oil for deep-frying to 350 degrees. Slip the pouches into the hot oil carefully and deep-fry for 3 minutes or until crispy.

YIELD: 6 *servings*. **Nutritional Facts Per Serving:** Calories 180; Total Fat 8g (Saturated Fat 1g); Cholesterol 0mg; Sodium 240mg; Total Carbohydrate 14g (Dietary Fiber 5g; Sugars 3g); Protein 17g

Nori-Maki Sushi (Veggie Seaweed Rolls) *(photo: page 79)*

Ingredients:

Vinegared Rice Flavoring:
3 tablespoons rice vinegar
$4^1/2$ teaspoons sugar
$1/4$ teaspoon salt

4 ounces fresh asparagus spears
2 ounces carrot
$1/4$ cup peanuts
2 (3-inch square) slices veggie tofu
cheese

Tezu Water:
4 cups cold water
$1/2$ cup rice vinegar

1 cup sushi rice
$1^3/4$ cups water
2 sheets Nori

Preparation:

- Prepare the Vinegared Rice Flavoring by combining the 3 tablespoons rice vinegar, sugar and salt in a small bowl, mix well and set aside.
- Discard the tough ends of the asparagus. Peel the carrot. Cut the asparagus and carrot into $1/4 \times 1/4 \times$ 8-inch sticks. Blanch the asparagus and carrot sticks in boiling water for just 2 minutes, drain and set aside.
- Grind the peanuts into powder.
- Cut the tofu cheese into $1/2$ inch wide strips and set aside.
- Prepare the Tezu Water by mixing 4 cups cold water with $1/2$ cup rice vinegar and set aside. Tezu is used for moistening your fingers and the knife to prevent the rice from sticking.

Procedure:

1. Combine the sushi rice and $1^3/4$ cups water in a 2-quart saucepan and boil over high heat for about 10 minutes. Reduce the heat to very low and cook, uncovered, until the height of the water disappears except for the steamed bubbles (called fish eyes) on the surface of the rice. Cover the pan and steam for 5 minutes.

2. Pour the Vinegared Rice Flavoring over the rice and mix thoroughly. Fan the rice while stirring in order to cool the rice quickly to bring out the pearl-like luster.

3. Keep hands moistened with Tezu Water while preparing sushi. Place 1 sheet of the Nori on a bamboo sushi mat aligning the edge of the Nori with the edge of the mat. Spread half the prepared sushi rice evenly over the Nori leaving the top inch of the Nori uncovered.

4. Line half the carrot sticks, tofu strips and asparagus side by side on the rice. Sprinkle half the peanut powder in a line next to the asparagus.

5. Roll the bamboo mat away from you to wrap the vegetables in the Nori and rice while pressing the mat tightly to compress the rice and Nori around the vegetables before releasing the bamboo mat. Moisten the open edge of the Nori with Tezu Water and press to seal.

6. Set the bamboo aside, dip a knife in the Tezu Water and cut the Nori-Maki into 8 pieces.

7. Repeat with the remaining ingredients.

YIELD: *4 servings.* **Nutritional Facts Per Serving:** Calories 290; Total Fat 6g (Saturated Fat 1g); Cholesterol 0mg; Sodium 560mg; Total Carbohydrate 50g (Dietary Fiber 1g; Sugars 5g); Protein 11g

Braised Yellow Partridge *(photo: page 79)*

Ingredients:

3 (9 × 10-inch) soybean curd skins

Stuffing Vegetables:
3 dried black mushrooms
1/4 cup bamboo shoots
1/4 cup carrot
1/2 cup yam paste (konnyaky), mashed
    yam or taro
1/4 cup baby corn

Seasoning Mix:
4 1/2 teaspoons light soy sauce
1 teaspoon sugar
1/4 teaspoon salt
1/2 teaspoon five-spice powder
1 teaspoon sesame oil
Dash of black or white pepper

Sauce:
1 cup water
2 teaspoons soy sauce
1 teaspoon sesame chili oil
Pinch each of sugar, salt and pepper

1 teaspoon cornstarch
1 tablespoon water
1 slice fresh gingerroot, minced
1 tablespoon vegetable oil
1 egg, beaten
4 to 6 cups peanut oil for deep-frying
10 ounces fresh spinach
1 tablespoon vegetable oil

Preparation:

- Cut the soybean curd skins into halves to make six 4 1/2 × 10-inch rectangles.
- Prepare the Stuffing Vegetables by soaking the mushrooms in boiling water for 15 minutes; drain, squeeze dry and discard the stems. Cut the mushroom caps, bamboo shoots and carrot into thin shreds and set aside. Chop the yam paste and baby corn finely and set aside.
- Prepare the Seasoning Mix by combining the ingredients, mix well and set aside.
- Blend the Sauce ingredients and set aside.
- Dissolve the cornstarch in 1 tablespoon water and set aside.

Procedure:

1. Heat a wok. Stir-fry the gingerroot in 1 tablespoon vegetable oil until fragrant. Add the mushrooms, bamboo shoots and carrot and stir-fry for several seconds. Add the yam paste, baby corn and the Seasoning Mix. Stir-fry for several seconds and set aside.
2. Spread beaten egg evenly over the soybean curd skin. Add 3 tablespoons of the Stuffing Vegetables and roll up to enclose the filling in a cylinder, twisting the ends and tying a knot in the center. Shape the ends to resemble a bird. Repeat process.
3. Heat the peanut oil to 350 degrees. Slip the partridges into the hot oil carefully, deep-fry until golden brown and drain on paper towels. Arrange the partridges in the center of a platter.
4. Stir-fry the spinach in 1 tablespoon vegetable oil for several seconds. Surround the partridges with the spinach.
5. Bring the Sauce mixture to a boil in the wok. Stir in the cornstarch mixture and cook until thickened, stirring constantly. Pour the sauce over the partridges and spinach and serve immediately.

If the soybean curd skins are dry, dip the skins in water and lay flat, then cover with a moist cloth to prevent drying.

YIELD: *6 servings.* **Nutritional Facts Per Serving:** Calories 160; Total Fat 11g (Saturated Fat 1.5g); Cholesterol 0mg; Sodium 350mg; Total Carbohydrate 12g (Dietary Fiber 2g; Sugars 1g); Protein 8g

Five-Fragrant Pressed Tofu Stir-Fried with Vegetables *(photo: page 80)*

Ingredients:

8 ounces five-fragrant pressed
  spiced tofu
1 cup canned golden mushrooms
$1/2$ cup carrot
$1/2$ cup celery
2 slices fresh gingerroot
2 dried red chili peppers
2 tablespoons vegetable oil
2 tablespoons dark soy sauce
1 teaspoon sugar
$1/4$ teaspoon salt
1 teaspoon sesame oil
Dash of black or white pepper

Preparation:

- Cut the tofu into $1/4 \times 1/2 \times 1 1/2$-inch slices and set aside.
- Drain the mushrooms, pat dry with a paper towel and set aside.
- Peel the carrot, cut into thin diagonal slices and then into $1/4 \times 1/3 \times 2$-inch shreds. Peel the stringy skin from the celery, cut lengthwise into halves and then diagonally into shreds the same size as the carrot.
- Mince the gingerroot. Cut the ends from the chili peppers, tap out the seeds and cut lengthwise into thin shreds.

Procedure:

1. Heat a wok. Add the vegetable oil. Add the gingerroot and chili peppers and stir-fry until fragrant.
2. Add the tofu, soy sauce, sugar and salt. Stir-fry for several seconds. Add the carrot, celery and golden mushrooms and stir-fry for several seconds. Stir in the sesame oil and pepper.
3. Serve the hot tofu mixture over steamed rice or freshly cooked noodles.

YIELD: *4 servings.* **Nutritional Facts Per Serving:** Calories 200; Total Fat 14g (Saturated Fat 1.5g); Cholesterol 0mg; Sodium 490mg; Total Carbohydrate 12g (Dietary Fiber 2g; Sugars 2g); Protein 11g

Steamed Brown Rice

Ingredients:

1 cup brown rice
$2 3/4$ cups cold water

Procedure:

1. Presoak the brown rice by covering with cold water and letting stand for 30 minutes. Drain well.
2. Combine the brown rice and $2 3/4$ cups cold water in a 2-quart saucepan.
3. Heat, uncovered, over high heat for about 10 minutes or until the mixture comes to a boil. Reduce the heat to medium-low and simmer for 25 minutes or until the water is almost absorbed. Reduce the heat to the lowest setting and cover the saucepan. Let stand over the low heat for 10 minutes before serving.

YIELD: *4 servings.* **Nutritional Facts Per Serving:** Calories 110; Total Fat 1g (Saturated Fat 0g); Cholesterol 0mg; Sodium 5mg; Total Carbohydrate 24g (Dietary Fiber 1g; Sugars 0g); Protein 2g

If you wish to increase the amount of brown rice, the amount of water should be a little more than just proportionally increased because the brown rice takes longer to cook and soften than white rice. Use $1 1/4$ cups brown rice with $3 1/2$ cups cold water.

Sesame Glutinous Rice Balls (photo: page 80)

Ingredients:

1 cup white sesame seeds

Dough:

2 cups glutinous rice flour

6 tablespoons sugar

3/4 cup water

1/2 cup sweet red bean paste

6 cups peanut or soybean oil for deep-frying

Preparation:

- Soak the sesame seeds in boiling water for 30 minutes. Drain well, spread on a tray and set aside.
- Prepare the Dough by mixing the glutinous rice flour and sugar in a bowl. Stir in the water gradually. Knead until smooth.

Procedure:

1. Shape the Dough into a long cylinder and cut into 20 equal portions. Roll each portion into a 2-inch circle.
2. Place 1 teaspoon red bean paste in the center of each circle, bring the edges together to enclose the filling, seal and shape into a ball. Dip the ball in water and roll in the sesame seeds to coat.
3. Heat the oil for deep-frying to 375 degrees. Add the balls to the hot oil carefully and deep-fry for 5 minutes or until golden. Drain on paper towels and serve immediately.

YIELD: 10 *servings*. **Nutritional Facts Per Serving:** Calories 310; Total Fat 13g (Saturated Fat 2g); Cholesterol 0mg; Sodium 50mg; Total Carbohydrate 44g (Dietary Fiber 4g; Sugars 8g); Protein 6g

The glutinous rice balls will become hard when cold. To soften, wrap the balls in a wet paper towel and microwave for 1 minute.

Arhat's Feast (Lo-Han Jai) *(photo: page 80)*

This is the most popular banquet dish served at the Buddhist temple. It is traditionally offered first to Lo-Hans, who are the enshrined minor gods in the temple. This dish is truly gourmet in taste and nutritious with a wide range of dried and fresh vegetables.

Ingredients:

12 ounces spoon cabbage (Ching-Chiang Tsai)
3 dried black mushrooms
6 slices carrot
4 baby corn
1/4 cup bamboo shoots
2 tablespoons hair seaweed
1 teaspoon cornstarch
1 teaspoon water
2 tablespoons vegetable oil
2 slices fresh gingerroot, minced
2 tablespoons soy sauce
1 teaspoon sugar
1 teaspoon sesame oil
1 cup water
1/4 cup straw mushrooms
1/2 cup gingko nuts
1/2 cup lotus nuts
1/3 cup yam paste
1 cup wheat gluten puffs

Preparation:

- Cut the ends from the spoon cabbage, separate the stems and trim the green leaves. Rinse the leaves, drain, pat dry and set aside.
- Soak the black mushrooms in boiling water to cover for 15 minutes. Drain, squeeze dry, discard the stems, cut the caps into thirds and set aside.
- Cut the carrots into fancy slices such as flowers and set aside. Cut the baby corn lengthwise into halves and set aside. Shred the bamboo shoots.
- Soak the hair seaweed in warm water for 5 minutes. Drain, pat dry and set aside.
- Dissolve the cornstarch in 1 teaspoon water and set aside.

Procedure:

1. Bring a generous amount of water in a 2-quart saucepan to a boil. Blanch the cabbage leaves briefly, just long enough to soften, drain and set aside.
2. Heat a wok. Add the vegetable oil and gingerroot and stir-fry until fragrant. Add the black mushrooms, carrots, baby corn and bamboo shoots and stir-fry for several seconds.
3. Add the soy sauce, sugar and sesame oil and mix well.
4. Add the 1 cup water, straw mushrooms, gingko nuts, lotus nuts, yam paste, wheat gluten puffs and the hair seaweed and mix well. Cover the wok and bring to a boil.
5. Stir the cornstarch mixture into the wok and cook until thickened, stirring constantly.
6. Line a serving platter with the spoon cabbage leaves and pour the hot vegetable mixture on top. Serve immediately with steamed rice or freshly cooked noodles.

YIELD: *6 servings.* **Nutritional Facts Per Serving:** Calories 150; Total Fat 6g (Saturated Fat .5g); Cholesterol 0mg; Sodium 250mg; Total Carbohydrate 22g (Dietary Fiber 1g; Sugars 2g); Protein 4g

Steamed Acorn Squash Bowls *(photo: page 80)*

Acorn squash is called southern squash in Chinese. It is the product of Southwestern provinces in China. This recipe can also be made with one Chinese winter melon but that is not readily available.

Ingredients:

2 acorn squash
1 teaspoon salt
1 cup hard tofu or soy meats
1 cup lotus nuts
8 straw mushrooms or
    2 dried black mushrooms
4 teaspoons finely chopped
    water chestnuts
4 teaspoons finely chopped
    bamboo shoots
$1/4$ cup frozen green peas and carrots
2 slices fresh gingerroot, minced
4 teaspoons light soy sauce
1 teaspoon sugar
1 teaspoon sesame oil

Preparation:

- Cut the squash into halves with a sharp cleaver. Trim enough from the bottoms to flatten the points and allow the 4 bowls to sit securely. Discard the seeds and scoop out some of the pulp to form a bowl. Rub the inside of each bowl with $1/4$ teaspoon salt and set aside.
- Cut the tofu into $1/3$-inch cubes and divide the tofu among the squash bowls. Add $1/4$ cup lotus nuts to each bowl.
- Cube the straw mushrooms and set aside. (If using black mushrooms, soak in boiling water to cover for 15 minutes, drain and squeeze dry, discard the stems and cut the caps into small pieces.)

Procedure:

1. Fill the bottom of a steamer at least $1/3$ full with water and bring to a boil.
2. Place the acorn squash bowls on an oiled steam rack over the boiling water. Cover and steam for 20 minutes.
3. Open the steamer and divide the mushrooms, water chestnuts, bamboo shoots and green peas and carrots among the squash bowls. Sprinkle with the gingerroot, soy sauce, sugar and sesame oil.
4. Cover the steamer and continue steaming over high heat for 10 minutes longer. Serve immediately.
5. Squash bowls may be further divided when served.

YIELD: *6 servings.* **Nutritional Facts Per Serving:** Calories 170; Total Fat 5g (Saturated Fat 1g); Cholesterol 0mg; Sodium 590mg; Total Carbohydrate 26g (Dietary Fiber 4g; Sugars 1g); Protein 9g

Menu Planning

Most of the recipes in this cookbook, when accompanied by steamed rice, will yield approximately four to six servings. However, this does not necessarily mean that the one dish alone will feed four to six people, as the Chinese tend to eat smaller servings of multiple dishes in the family style.

What is important in planning a menu is to select a combination of dishes that provides a well-balanced mix of meat and/or seafood, vegetables and grains. It is also important to have steamed rice accompanying most of the dishes, especially stir-fry dishes. Easily digested and nutritional, rice is the staple food to Asians. In some cases, fried rice will be substituted for steamed rice, however, noodles usually do not replace rice unless a noodle recipe is the only main dish served (as in Menu #6 on page 164).

The beginner cook should allow for about 30 minutes more than the estimated preparation and cooking time listed for each menu. The preparation, referring mostly to cutting and slicing, is a big part of the time and effort in Chinese cooking. The more you practice at using a cleaver, the faster your cutting speed will become.

With more experience, you will also learn to organize what dish to prepare first for greatest efficiency. For example, in Menu 3 (page 163) you should start by slicing the vegetables and meats for the stir-fry dish (Chinese Cabbage in Chicken Sauce). Then prepare and cook the Clear Steamed Fish which takes 20 minutes to cook. During that time, prepare and cook the steamed rice (15 minutes cooking time). While the fish and rice are steaming, complete the preparation and cooking of the stir-fry dish. Then all three dishes will finish cooking at the same time.

The Chinese regularly drink hot tea with their meals. The variety chosen often depends on complementing the flavor of the dishes as well as personal preference. In the sample menus below, I've included a recommendation for a tea that is well-suited to the selections.

Simple Meal for Two

The following menus are suggested for a simple meal for two people.

Menu 1

- Shredded Beef with Green Pepper (page 27)
  or
  Chicken with Cashew Nuts (page 29)
- Steamed White or Brown Rice (pages 26, 158)
- Fresh Orange Slices
- Oolong or Chinese Restaurant Tea
  Preparation & Cooking Time: 30 Minutes

Menu 2

- Assorted Three-Shreds Cold Plate (page 62)
- Fried Rice (page 35)
- Fresh Fruits
- Oolong Tea
  Preparation & Cooking Time: 40 Minutes

Menu 3

- Clear Steamed Fish (page 40)
- Chinese Cabbage in Chicken Sauce (page 38)
- Steamed White or Brown Rice (pages 26, 158)
- Green Tea
  Preparation & Cooking Time: 35 Minutes

Weekend Dinner for Two

The following menus are suggested for a weekend dinner for two people.

Menu 4

- Sweet and Sour Pork (page 30)
- Steamed White or Brown Rice (pages 26, 158)
- Almond Float (page 31)
- Oolong Tea
  Preparation & Cooking Time: 60 Minutes

Tip: The Almond Float can be made ahead of time. For two, cut the amount of fruit used in half.

Menu 5

- Assorted Three-Shreds Cold Plate (page 62)
- Kung Pao Chicken Ding (page 61)
- Steamed White or Brown Rice (pages 26, 158)
- Ginseng Oolong Tea or Black Tea
  Preparation & Cooking Time: 50 Minutes

Menu 6

- Cantonese Barbecue Roast Pork (page 41)
- Roast Pork Lo-Mein (page 42)
- Fresh Orange Slices
- Jasmine or Orange Ginger Tea
  Preparation & Cooking Time: 60 Minutes

Tip: The Cantonese Barbecue Roast Pork and Roast Pork Lo-Mein recipes may be cut in half for two people. For a dinner for four, you can either increase the size of the recipes above, or add another dish.

Simple Menu for Four

The following menus are examples of simple meals for four people.

Menu 7

- Egg Drop Soup (page 28)
- Chicken with Cashew Nuts (page 29)
- Steamed White or Brown Rice (pages 26, 158)
- Almond Float (page 31)
- Oolong Tea
  Preparation & Cooking Time: 60 Minutes

Tip: The Almond Float can be made ahead of time. If making your own clear stock for Egg Drop Soup, this can also be prepared in advance.

Weekend Dinner for Four

The following menu would be good for a weekend dinner for four people.

Menu 8

- Clear Steamed Fish (page 40)
- Fried Rice (page 35)
- Mongolian Lamb with Hot Sauce (page 116)
- Chinese Almond Cookies (page 97)
- Oolong Tea
  Preparation & Cooking Time: 1^1/$_2$ Hours

Tip: The Chinese Almond Cookies can be made up to two days ahead.

- -

Dinner Party for Six

A dinner party for six people might feature the following menu.

Menu 9

- Cantonese Barbecue Roast Pork (page 41)
- Roast Pork Lo-Mein (page 42)
- Four Kinds of Braised Vegetables (page 52)
- Lovers Shrimp (page 134)
- Steamed White or Brown Rice (pages 26, 158)
- Chinese Almond Cookies (page 97)
- Oolong Tea
  Preparation & Cooking Time: 2½ Hours

Tip: The Chinese Almond Cookies can be made up to two days ahead.

Special Occasion Dinner Party for Eight or More

A dinner party for eight or more on a special occasion might feature the following menu.

Menu 10

- Hot and Sour Soup (page 54)
- Egg Rolls (page 34)
- Lemon Chicken (page 49)
- Beef in Oyster Sauce (page 50)
- Fried Rice (page 35)
  or
  Steamed White or Brown Rice (pages 26, 158)
- Dan-Dan Mein (page 150)
- Dry-Fried String Beans (page 131)
- Almond Float (page 31)
- Different varieties of tea including Green, Jasmine and/or Oolong
  Preparation & Cooking Time: 5 Hours

Tips: The Almond Float can be made ahead. For the Egg Rolls, the stuffing can be prepared in advance, or the wrapped Egg Rolls can be partially fried the day before with a quick heat up in the deep-fryer before serving. If possible, get help wrapping the egg rolls. All the meats and vegetables in every dish can be sliced a day ahead and kept refrigerated. These are the most time-consuming tasks.

Peking Opera Company Catering

Next I've included the menus that I used when catering the meals for the Peking Opera Company during their two-week performance at the Kennedy Center in 1980. The company had 75 members, and the dishes were served banquet-style, with each table of ten receiving all courses. In addition to a sample lunch (the main meal for the day) and late night supper (light snack eaten after their performance at 9:45 p.m.), this menu illustrates the more ambitious and celebrated dishes that are usually prepared for special occasions, as in the Welcome and Farewell Party banquets. These banquet dishes are often served on holidays, such as Chinese New Year, and require more time and skill, however, the results are well worth the effort for these very memorable events. Varieties of Chinese hot tea are served with each meal.

Welcome Banquet (September 1, 1980)

Authentic Chinese ten-course lunch served banquet-style, serving ten.

Menu 11

- Cold Appetizer Platter: Soy-Bean Sauce Pork Szechuan-Style (page 122)
- Hot Appetizer: Egg Rolls, Shanghai and Canton-Style (page 34)
- Red Cooked Chicken with Spinach
  (see Red Cooking, page 12)
- Pearl Balls (page 51)
- Hot and Spicy Scallops in Sweet and Sour Sauce (page 83)
  (substitute scallops for fish)
- Fragrant Crispy Duck with Steamed Lotus Leaf Buns (pages 123, 124)
- Winter Melon with Assorted Treasures Soup
- Shredded Beef with Assorted Vegetables (page 27)
  (add your choice of vegetables)
- Mongolian Lamb with Hot Sauce (page 116)
- Eight-Treasures Rice Pudding (page 89)

At a formal banquet which consists of a ten-course meal, the most celebrated dish (like Fragrant Crispy Duck or Peking Duck) is usually served at the half-way point, just before the light dessert (like Almond Float). The last course is usually the soup or the heavier dessert.

Sample Lunch

Six authentic dishes that vary day to day.

Menu 12

- Taiwanese Fried Pork Meatballs (page 90)
- Chinese Cabbage in Chicken Sauce (page 38)
- Chicken with Cashew Nuts (page 29)
- Shredded Beef with Green Pepper (page 27)
- Shrimp Fried Rice (page 35) (omit the meat and use 1 cup shrimp)
- Hot and Sour Soup (page 54)

Sample Late-Night Supper

Two dishes that vary day to day, served with bread, buns or rolls.

Menu 13

- Cantonese Barbecue Roast Pork (page 41)
- Dan-Dan Mein (page 150)

Add a dessert, and a generous assortment of fresh fruit.

Farewell Party Banquet (September 15, 1980)

Authentic Chinese ten-course lunch served banquet style for ten people.

Menu 14

- Cold Appetizer Platter: Assorted Three-Shreds Cold Plate (page 62)
- Hot Appetizer: Chiao-Tzu Northern Dumplings (page 44)
- Shredded Beef with Yu-Xiang Sauce (page 114)
- Clear Steamed Fish (page 40)
- Lemon Chicken (page 49)
- Peking Duck with Mandarin Thin Pancakes (pages 46, 106)
- Almond Float (page 31)
- Butterfly Shrimp (page 37)
- Twice-Cooked Pork (page 119)
- Egg Drop Soup (page 28)

How to set a Chinese Banquet table:

Use a big round table that seats ten people. For each diner, set a rice bowl, a medium-sized salad plate, and a dip dish (for soy sauce or other sauces). Set a pair of chopsticks on a chopstick rest and a porcelain spoon on the dip dish. Set a tea cup and a napkin beside each place setting.

Index

Index

Index of Recipes

Index of Recipes

The Art of The Chinese Cookery

The Chinese Cookery, Inc.
14209 Sturtevant Road
Silver Spring, Maryland 20905

Please send _____ copies of *The Art of The Chinese Cookery* @ $26.95 ea. $ _____

Add 5% Maryland sales tax @ $1.35 ea. . . . . $ _____

Add shipping and handling @ $4.95 ea. . . . . $ _____

Total . . . . $ _____

Bill To:

Name _____

Street Address _____

City _____ State _____ Zip _____

Telephone _____

Method of Payment: [   ] MasterCard   [   ] VISA

[   ] Check payable to The Chinese Cookery, Inc.

Account Number _____ Expiration Date _____

Signature _____

Send A Gift To:

Name _____

Street Address _____

City _____ State _____ Zip _____

Photocopies will be accepted.

Order Information

Telephone:
(301) 236-5311

Fax:
(240) 597-7515

Email:
ChineseCookery@aol.com

If you want the best,
Shih (pronounced "she") is the one!
—**Abe Przygoda**

Confucious is reputed to have refused…
a meal unless it was properly prepared and
presented. Joan…taught us…so that
he would have eaten and enjoyed.
—**Melvin Bergman, Attorney-at-Law**
and JoIna Bergman

Joan's classes…are a demonstration that good
eating can be healthful eating—vegetarian
recipes that are flavorful, quick and easy.
—**Peter Greenwald, M.D.**
and Harriet Greenwald

A culinary tour of Chinese cooking…
—**Richard A. Roepke**

The classes are great for all ages.
—**Mary A. Erdle**

Joan brings the Orient to you!
—**Jenny Clagett**

Each recipe is an exciting new discovery.
—**Daniel T. Brooking**

Authentic Chinese recipes masterfully
re-created.
—**Joyce Uy**

A Chinese friend was shocked to eat such
quality food cooked by a non-Chinese.
—**Bob Fustero**

My friends and family are impressed with
the recipes and techniques I've learned.
—**David Erickson**

Butterfly Shrimp 37

Lemon Chicken 49 (Especially the
marinade

Sweet + Sour Pork 30
+ Make this by roasting
Pork, then finish the
roast finish by basting
the roast with sweet +
sour pork.

Lobster Shrimp 134

FISH (Clear Steamed Fish" P.
Especially the best with
circled.